KIDS INVENTING!

A Handbook for Young Inventors

SUSAN CASEY

JOSSEY-BASS
A Wiley Imprint
www.josseybass.com

To the memory of my mom and dad, Joan and Tom Casey,
and my brother Tom. Also to my brothers and sisters:
Patsy, Mike, Kevin, Jim, and Katie.

This book is printed on acid-free paper. ∞

Copyright © 2005 by Susan Mary Casey. All rights reserved

Published by John Wiley & Sons, Inc., Hoboken, New Jersey
Published simultaneously in Canada

Design and composition by Navta Associates, Inc.

For general information about our other products and services, please contact our Customer Care Department within the United States at (800) 762-2974, outside the United States at (317) 572-3993 or fax (317) 572-4002.

Wiley also publishes its books in a variety of electronic formats. Some content that appears in print may not be available in electronic books. For more information about Wiley products, visit our web site at www.wiley.com.

Library of Congress Cataloging-in-Publication Data:

Casey, Susan (Susan Mary)
    Kids inventing : a handbook for young inventors / Susan Casey.
        p. cm.
    Includes index.
    ISBN-13 978-0-471-66086-6 (pbk.)
    ISBN-10 0-471-66086-8 (pbk.)
    1. Inventions—Juvenile literature. 2. Children as inventors—Juvenile literature. I. Title.

T339.C355 2005
608—dc22

Printed in the United States of America

10 9 8 7 6 5 4

Contents

Foreword by Nicholas D. Frankovits and Leila Gay Evans   vii

Acknowledgments   ix

Introduction   1

1   Getting an Idea   3

Look for a Problem to Solve   4

Break Problems into Smaller Parts   5

Think about Improving Something You Already Enjoy   7

Think about Solving a Community Problem   11

Think about the Needs of Others   13

Find an Idea Through Research   15

Find a Use for Something You Discover   18

Is Your Idea an Invention?   20

Activities   20

**2   Keeping a Journal or an Inventor's Log and
Writing a Report   23**

Logs and Journals   23

Reports   34

Inventor's Logs, Journals, and Reports as Part of a Display   35

Activities   36

3 Making a Model 37

    Start with a Sketch 39

    Make a List of Materials 39

    List the Tools You Will Need 40

    Estimate Costs 41

    Inventory Your Skills and Acquire Others 41

    Set up a Workshop 42

    Ask for Help and Be Safe 43

    Make a Scale Model 45

    Activities 46

4 Naming Your Invention 50

    Name Your Invention after Yourself 50

    Name Your Invention for What It Does 51

    Use Word Tricks in Naming Your Invention 52

    Name Your Invention for Its Sound 53

    Name Your Invention for Its Feel 53

    Give Your Invention a Catchy Name 54

    Activities 56

5 Participating in Competitions, Programs, and Camps 57

    What You Can Gain by Entering an Invention Contest 58

    Preparing for Competition 58

    Camps 65

    Activities 65

6 Inventing as a Team 66

    Teamwork Calls for Cooperation and Compromise 66

    Small Teams 70

    Large Teams 71

    Activities 73

7 Learning with a Mentor 74

    Mentors Are Guides 74

    School Mentor Programs 77

    Mentors from the Business Community 78

    Activities 81

8   Patenting an Invention   82

How Inventions Are Patented   82

The Patent Search   83

Types of Patents   85

Patent Applications   90

Patent Infringement   91

Activities   94

9   Registering a Trademark   95

Trademarks Are All Around You   95

Trademark Symbols   95

Types of Trademarks   96

Applying for a Trademark   97

Trademarks instead of Patents   98

Activities   101

10   Manufacturing, Packaging, and Selling an Invention   102

Product Development   105

Find the Right Company to Manufacture Your Invention   109

Selling Your Invention   109

Licensing Your Invention   111

Activities   114

Appendix A: Suggested Reading   116

Appendix B: Useful Web Sites   117

Appendix C: Invention Competitions, Programs, and Camps   119

Index   129

Photo Credits   134

Foreword

The idea of being an inventor may seem impossible to you, yet everyone is born with innate curiosity and a desire to explore. Children discover at different rates, based on their physical surroundings. New sense impressions—sights, smells, tastes, and sounds—provide them with increased awareness of the world. Exposure to new ideas by their families and teachers also expands their creative possibilities.

Invention is the result of combining elements that people already possess with new, unexpected elements, which allows or even forces individuals to think "differently" about what already exists. An invention can be the outcome of a "Eureka!" moment, when an idea simply springs into an inventor's mind. However, this type of invention is usually built upon a foundation of past knowledge, events, and memories. An invention can also result from years of research and trial and error.

You already have the characteristics and the qualities of an inventor. Yet learning to "rethink" your reality, the world around you, requires that you have confidence to think outside the box and look at your environment in a new, unique way. Sometimes taking this risk is frightening, yet great inventors throughout history have been willing to break the paradigms of their structured worlds.

Once your imagination has been tweaked and you are given tools to work with, nothing can stop you from pursuing your goals. Whether you become a true inventor, as the world defines it, or you keep your creations to yourself will depend upon your confidence and the help you get from parents, teachers, and other adults. We all hold within us a universe of possibilities. A budding Thomas Edison could live right next door or be one of your classmates. Who knows? You yourself might become the world's greatest inventor. There are no limits to what our minds can imagine.

Kids Inventing!: A Handbook for Young Inventors will help you on your way. It explains the steps of inventing and marketing your creations, points you to sources of additional information, and provides stories of young inventors who are probably not that different from you. This book can help you to become a true inventor.

At the Partnership for America's Future, Inc., we envisioned the need to preserve and enshrine the great inventions of America's students in a museum framework. We realized that although many young inventors were recognized at local, state, regional, and even national levels through various contests, exhibits, and competitions, once the initial award had been given, there was no enduring legacy. Since its establishment in 1996, the National Gallery for America's Young Inventors has celebrated the inventiveness of six of America's youths each year. By recognizing and preserving these inventions, we also celebrate the contributions of all young inventors.

If you would like to view what other young inventors have done, visit our Web site at www.pafinc.com and click on "National Gallery for America's Young Inventors."

Nicholas D. Frankovits, Executive Director
Leila Gay Evans, Assistant Executive Director
National Gallery for America's Young Inventors

Acknowledgments

Writing a book of this nature requires a lot of help and cooperation. I extend a bountiful thanks to all of the young inventors and their parents and teachers who were so kind in sharing their stories with me. I am indebted to my editor, Kate Bradford, for her vision, direction, and sagacity and especially for her understanding. Tremendous thanks to Kimberly Monroe-Hill and Constance Santisteban at Wiley, for their attention to detail. It wouldn't be a book without the efforts of my agents, Sheree Bykofsky and Janet Rosen. Ruth Nyblod, of the United States Patent and Trademark Office (USPTO), provided tremendous help, as did Katherine McDaniel, Esq. Thanks to Gay Evans, Nick Frankovits, and Sue Lyons, of the Partnership for America's Future, for so many things; to Kristin Finn, of the Lemelson-MIT Program; to Linda Heller, of ExploraVision; to Carol Simantz, on behalf of the Craftsman/NSTA Young Inventors Awards Program; to Clar Baldus, of Invent Iowa; Cathy MacDonald, of the Young Inventors Fair and Program in the Twin Cities metro area of Minnesota; and to Norm Goldstein, of By Kids For Kids, for all their suggestions and cooperation. Thanks as well to Pamela Riddle Bird, of the United Inventors Association, and Dr. Forrest Bird. Teachers Jon Hood, Bill Church, Richard Jones, and Rich Fasciano; coaches Kristen Haugen, Joan Hurd, Joe Ann Clark, and Janice Hansen; and mentor John McConnell provided me with much help and needed insights.

Many, many thanks for all the efforts of Cliff Tanner of Science Service; Judith Shellenberger and Stephanie Hallman of the Christopher Columbus Fellowship Foundation; Marie Gentile of the Siemens Westinghouse Competition in Math, Science & Technology; Kim Bratcher of Wild Planet Toys; Megan Brumagin of eCYBERMISSION; Kristen Greenaway of TOYchallenge; Katie Stack of the Discovery

Channel Young Scientist Challenge; Annie Wood of the Inventive Kids Around the World Contest; and Saki at SD Color Lab.

I would also like to thank Frank Tobin for his "seize the day" mind-set and for giving me travel opportunities to meet so many young inventors. Judith Maloney should be canonized for her efforts in helping me at the start of the process. And I am so grateful to Caroline Hatton, Rachelle Romberg Tuber, Mary Rose O'Leary, Michelle Markel, and Nancy Lamb for the generous gift of their time and scrutiny.

On a personal level, I am so grateful to the extended Ogren family for their enthusiasm and to all my friends who were continually supportive, especially Lou, Rachel, Susan, Anne, Denis, Mary, Hugo, Donvieve, Carrie, and members of the book club. Special thanks to Howard Katzman. Most of all, I want to thank my family, especially my dear nieces and nephews, for their love and support.

Introduction

Did you ever see kid inventors on TV or in the newspaper and think, "That could be me!" You're right—it could. Kids have been inventing for ages, making gadgets or toys or devising tools to make their chores easier. Most kids didn't even realize they were inventors. Yet some kids sold their creations, and others became famous because of them.

Today, more and more kids are inventing things. Maybe you've thought about being an inventor. Maybe you're already an inventor. Perhaps you've participated in a school invention fair or a national contest, yet you want to know more. What other contests can I enter? What's a patent? What's a trademark? Can kids really sell their inventions? How can I do that?

This book leads you through the steps of turning your ideas into realities, transforming you from a kid with a solution to a problem into an actual inventor. Perhaps you'll discover an aspect of inventing that really appeals to you—getting ideas, making a model, writing in your log, naming your invention, presenting your ideas to others, working as part of a team or with a mentor, or even selling your invention.

Let the kid inventors you'll read about in this book inspire you. They worked hard, and they had fun. Some made money. Some won scholarships. All of them were optimists. They believed that they could solve the problems they faced at different stages of inventing, and they experienced the joy of solving those problems and delighting, surprising, and astonishing others with the results.

Being a kid inventor has its own rewards, one of which is the thrill of saying, "I'm an inventor." Inventing is a series of steps, a journey of discovery. To begin your journey, just turn the page.

Getting an Idea

Imagine living in 1900. You would know about the lightbulb and the steamship. You could see fireworks shows and ride in a train. You could use a safety pin, invented in 1849, a cash register, invented in 1883, and a zipper, invented in 1893. But you would have to wait three years to see the Wright Brothers fly their airplane, ten years to listen to a radio broadcast, fifty-one years before you and your family could watch a black-and-white television, seventy-seven years to use a personal computer, and eighty-nine years to play a video game. Boy, things have changed—thanks to inventions.

All inventions begin with an idea. An inventor looks at an everyday problem and creates a solution. Inventors think about new ways to do things, and some of those inventors are kids.

Even before 1900, kids were inventing things. Here are two examples.

- In 1864, when he was fifteen years old, George Westinghouse worked in his father's factory, where he experimented with ways to improve steam engines. Four years later he gained a patent for a rotary steam engine.

- In 1850, twelve-year-old Mattie Knight of New Hampshire, a girl who was always using her tools to make playthings for her brothers, witnessed an accident at a cotton mill where her brothers worked. A piece of machinery broke off and injured one of the workers. In response, she invented a safety device that the mill owner used to prevent similar accidents. Over her lifetime, Mattie gained twenty-seven patents.

Inventor's Tip

"To get ideas, look at the problems in your life and try to figure out how they could be fixed."

—*Krysta Morlan, inventor of the Waterbike*

3

Inventions are new, and they are not obvious. In other words, not just anyone can dream up inventions. When people see an invention, they might say, "Wow, that's great! I've never seen that before. Maybe I could use it."

Some revolutionary inventions, such as the lightbulb, the radio, engines that power trains or automobiles, or the telephone, completely change the way we do things. Others, such as inline skates, the ballpoint pen, or binoculars, improve certain aspects of our lives.

Inventions take many forms. An invention can be an item with no moving parts, like a pencil. It can be a machine, such as an elevator, or a new variety of plant—for example, a tomato. It can be a design for something, such as a chair, or a new concept, like an ice cream cone. It can also be a process, a series of steps. The steps can lead to the production of a drug to fight cancer or other illnesses or to the recipe for a new kind of salad dressing. A process can even be the series of steps to play a game or program a computer.

Inventions that improve on existing inventions are called innovations. The bicycle, for example, is an old idea. Ancient Chinese drawings show two-wheeled vehicles. An Egyptian obelisk is carved with a hieroglyph of a man on a bar mounted on two wheels. When the modern bicycle was invented in 1790, it didn't have pedals. People moved the vehicle by pushing it with their feet. In 1839, when modern pedals were invented, bicycles became much more popular, but riding on wheels made only of metal was a bit rough. With the invention of air-filled tires in 1888, bikes became much more comfortable. Since then, there have been many more innovations in bicycles. Even as you read this, items that we use every day are being improved—everything from televisions and washing machines to tennis racquets and car engines.

Look for a Problem to Solve

What can you invent? How can you come up with ideas that lead to an invention? Thinking of ideas for an invention can be an everyday activity. All year long, we do things over and over again. We eat, sleep, do our chores, go to school, play sports, care for others, listen to music, use the computer, go to the store, talk on the phone, and send messages via computer. Each of our activities is an area that can benefit from inventions. In 1860, the future Sierra Club founder, John Muir, at age seventeen, invented a study desk that automatically turned the pages of a book. Muir displayed his well-crafted invention that year at the Wisconsin State Agricultural Fair.

You will most likely have ideas for inventions that solve problems in your daily life. You're an expert on your chores and on things your family likes or hates to do. You know what works well or doesn't, what's fun or hard. If you live on a farm, you're more likely than a city kid would be to invent something to help with farm chores. If you ride a bike or play soccer, football, or basketball, you may think of inventions related to sports. Kids who are crazy about music or computers usually focus their creativity on those areas. If your parents work in advertising, as plumbers or chemists, in construction, or at any other type of job, you probably know more than you

Brainstorming

Brainstorming is one way to come up with ideas for inventions. Brainstorming means to engage in organized, shared problem solving. You get together with your friends or classmates, pick a topic, and then throw out ideas about it: for example, ideas on how to simplify your chores or make it easier to carry things, or you could think up ideas for a new game. Even though brainstorming is defined as a shared activity, you can also brainstorm by yourself, even while you're involved in other things.

Throw out any idea, even if it sounds really crazy. A few decades ago, a kid was brainstorming and thought of an idea for a remote-controlled vacuum cleaner. It sounded impossible then, but today it exists. Let the ideas fly. Brainstorm about sports, toys, computers, the environment, or community problems. Think of things that concern your family or other families. Throw out ideas as soon as you think of them, then let more ideas come. Let one idea lead to another. Eventually, some of these ideas won't seem so crazy after all. Be sure to jot down all of the ideas in a log or a journal.

realize about these fields. Take advantage of the knowledge that's available in your own house or community.

When inventors look at the world around them and see a problem, they think about how to solve it. For example, Marion Donovan invented the first disposable diaper in 1951. You know the problem that this solved! No more washing dirty diapers. So, be aware of people's problems or needs when you think of ideas for inventions.

If you're like most kids, you'd like your chores to be easier. Think about these activities and the tools you use to perform them. Almost anything around the house can be improved—brooms, rakes, dishwashing sponges, book bags, shovels, or scissors. The list goes on and on.

Inventor's Tip

"Look for something to help out with everyday chores. I had to pick up gumballs every day, so I thought, Surely, there's an easier way."

—Lindsey Clement, 2001 inductee into the National Gallery for America's Young Inventors for the Gumball Machine

Break Problems into Smaller Parts

Problems can often be broken down into separate parts. The whole idea of feeding a pet or polishing the floor may seem like a hassle. You may not like anything about it, but what do you focus on to make it better? Think about it. What exactly is the most annoying aspect of feeding the dog, the cat, or the bird? Or of cleaning the floor? Is it that you don't like having to do it every day? Or that your dog or cat nudges you when you try to put food in the bowl? Maybe you don't like cleaning up afterward?

The Edible Pet Spoon

Suzanna Goodin was a first-grader at Hydro Elementary School in Hydro, Oklahoma, in 1987. She didn't like feeding her cats, Cinnamon and Ginger. The cat food stuck to the spoon and was hard to get off. When her twin brother, Sam, told her he was trying to invent something to enter in the Weekly Reader Invention Contest, she thought, What if I invent a spoon that I don't have to wash? What if I could make a spoon the cats could eat? She talked to her mom about it, then made a small spoon out of dough, and baked it. For her invention of the Edible Pet Spoon, Suzanna won the Grand Prize of the Weekly Reader Invention Contest in 1987. (This contest no longer exists, but many other contests have taken its place.) ■

Think about which part of an activity or a job is really the problem. Is the task boring, or does it take too long? Think of how you can make it go more quickly or make it fun. Is something too heavy to carry or too hard to reach? Focus on what might make it easier to carry or reach. Is it too messy? Think of ways to protect yourself from the mess or devise a cleaner way to do the same job. If you look at what annoys you most about the problem, you can focus on finding a specific solution.

Sit and Go

Have you ever had to wheel your suitcase for a long distance and you just wanted to sit down for a minute? Well, Renee Steinberg, of Brooklyn, New York, decided to do something about that. She invented Sit and Go, a folding chair attached to a rolling suitcase. It's a seat for travelers. She was a 2004 National Finalist in the Craftsman/NSTA Young Inventors Awards Program. ■

Renee Steinberg sits on her invention, the Sit and Go.

Grip Stick

Alyssa Zordan was a seventh-grader at Torrington Middle School in Torrington, Connecticut, when her science teacher, Mr. Fasciano, challenged her and her classmates to become inventors. Alyssa was thinking about the assignment when she noticed that her grandmother almost slipped as she walked with her cane up the steps to Alyssa's house. She also thought about how her brother's running shoes had spikes on the bottom so that he could get a good grip on the track as he ran. She put the two ideas together to create a retractable metal tube with spikes on the bottom that fit over a cane to help the elderly walk on ice. She called it the Grip Stick. She designed it, then her dad, a shop teacher, helped her build it. During the process she used a metal lathe and a milling machine, and her dad helped her with welding. "I just wanted to win the school contest," said Alyssa. And she did. She also won first place in the grade 6 through 8 division of the 2004 Craftsman/NSTA Young Inventors Awards Program. ■

THE CRAFTSMAN/NSTA YOUNG INVENTORS AWARDS PROGRAM, which began in 1996, challenges students in the United States and its territories in grades 2 through 8 to invent or modify a tool that makes life easier. It is designed to teach students the scientific principles of how tools operate, to introduce them to working with tools, and to enable them to develop practical solutions to everyday problems. Students must work independently to create and conceive their tool inventions, though they may have guidance from an adult. Each student documents his or her progress in an inventor's log and includes a diagram of the tool and a photograph of the student using the tool. The contest is sponsored by Craftsman, a Sears-exclusive tool brand, in conjunction with the National Science Teachers Association.

Think about Improving Something You Already Enjoy

Kids have all sorts of hobbies and interests. Think about your hobby or about the sport you play. In 1963, while in his junior high school wood shop class, eighth-grader Tom Sims thought of something he liked to do. He made a ski-board, attached straps, and headed for the snow. Eventually, he formed a company to manufacture it and helped to launch the sport of snowboarding.

Sports are a great area for invention. Think about what aspect of a sport is scary or unsafe or hard to do. Can you imagine something to make it easier or more fun? Or a safety device that would make it better?

The Trahan Torso Protector

At the Invent Iowa 2003 State Invention Convention, fourth-grader Kevin Trahan, of Dubuque, Iowa, submitted a life jacket–like vest that he called the Trahan Torso Protector. "A lot of kids are scared of the ball," said Kevin, "but with this, they won't be." Kids playing baseball would wear his vest to protect their chests from balls that are hit or thrown at them. "If they wear it," said Kevin, "it doesn't interfere with their swing, and if a ball hits them right over the heart, they don't get hurt or die." ■

> INVENT IOWA, coordinated by the Connie Belin & Jacqueline N. Blank International Center for Gifted Education and Talent Development, is an annual statewide invention program open to students in grades K through 12 who live in Iowa. Over thirty thousand students participate each year in the program, which began in 1987.

The Retractable Bicycle Fender

Kevin Sellars, of Huntington Beach, California, was a seventh-grader when he created the Retractable Bicycle Fender. Kevin knew that many kids who performed jumps and tricks didn't want fenders on their bikes. Yet Kevin had watched a bicyclist get a very muddy shirt after riding a bike with no fender through a puddle. Kevin worked with his godfather, Ben Viola, in Viola's machine shop to make a retractable fender. The four sections of Kevin's fender pull out when fully extended. He was a winner in the 2003 Invent America! Student Invention Contest. ■

> INVENT AMERICA! is a nonprofit educational program of the United States Patent Model Foundation. The program, aimed at grades K through 8, was launched in 1987. Schools or families can purchase curriculum kits that include handbooks with step-by-step instructions for developing an invention project. Kits also include contest entry forms for the national Invent America! Student Invention Contest.

Music is an important part of many people's lives. Some people listen to music, and others play it. Some want to invent instruments that make new sounds. Many would like to make their instruments easier to play. Yet others turn their thoughts to inventing.

The Automated Page-Replacing Contrivance

When Christopher Cho, of East Setauket, New York, was in high school, he played the viola, studied at the Juilliard School of Music Pre-College division, won the viola concerto competition in 1995, and performed solo with the Juilliard Pre-College Symphony Orchestra. To make it easier to turn pages of music without interrupting his performances, Christopher invented the battery-powered Automated Page-Replacing Contrivance. When he pressed on a foot pedal, a spring turned and the top sheet of his music would drop, allowing him to see the next page and to keep playing.

He got the idea by watching how food snacks dropped in vending machines. He was a 1996 inductee into the National Gallery for America's Young Inventors. ■

> The purpose of the **NATIONAL GALLERY FOR AMERICA'S YOUNG INVENTORS** is to preserve and promote great inventions produced by America's youths. Young people in grades K through 12 who have won a national contest, have gained a patent, or have a product that is being marketed are eligible to apply. Since 1996, six students have been inducted annually. Information about them and their inventions can be viewed at www.pafinc.com.

Let's not leave out toys. There's always room for more toys, and some kids are busy thinking up ideas for new ones.

The Light Hand

Shahid Minipara, of San Francisco, came up with the idea of a toy that puts lights on the ends of your fingers, so he made a drawing of his idea and entered the drawing into Wild Planet Toys Inc.'s Kid Inventor Challenge. The company liked the idea, made it into a product called Light Hand, and sold it in stores across the country. On the package is a quote by Shahid: "It's cool to have lights at your fingertips, huh?" ■

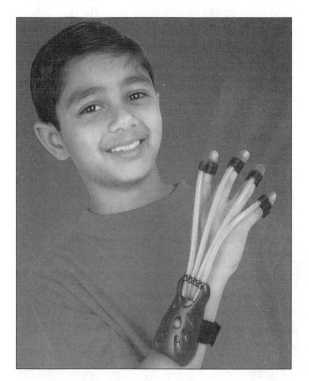

Shahid Minipara wearing his invention, the Light Hand.

> **THE KID INVENTOR CHALLENGE**, hosted by Wild Planet Toys Inc., is a contest open to kids age twelve and younger who live in the United States or Canada (excluding Quebec). Kids are asked to invent their own toys by drawing pictures of their toys and writing a brief description. Some kids who enter are selected to be toy consultants for a year. This means that they get lots of free toys and get to give their opinion on them. A select few kids have their ideas for toys made and sold by Wild Planet.

Boogie-2-Boogie

Four Southern California kids formed a team called the Wave Riders when they created Boogie-2-Boogie, a wave-riding board for two. It's fun but also safe for kids. Attached to the nose is a light that's controlled by a transmitter held by a parent on shore. If it's time for the kids to come out of the water, the parent keys the transmitter, which triggers a flashing red light. That alerts the wave-riding duo. The team included sisters Amy, 13, and Alyssa Hansen, 10, and their friends Nicholas Johnsen, 12, and his sister Kaycee, 10. They were the TOYchallenge 2004 winners. Hasbro, one of the sponsors, made action figures of the team members as prizes. ■

> TOYCHALLENGE asks kids in grades 5 through 8 to form teams of three to eight members (at least half of each team must consist of girls) and work with an adult coach (eighteen years of age or older). They are asked to create an interactive toy or a game. The astronaut Sally Ride brought Smith College, Hasbro, Sigma Xi, and Sally Ride Science together to launch this challenge to encourage teenagers, especially girls, to be interested in science, math, and engineering.

Maybe computers are your favorite hobby. There are plenty of opportunities to invent things that relate to computers. In the mid-1960s, when computers were large machines used only in offices, thirteen-year-old Steve Wozniak of Sunnyvale, California, built his own computer, a machine that could play tic-tac-toe. He was interested in electronics and was later president of the electronics club at Homestead High School. For the next ten years, he continued building computers in his garage, and in 1977, he presented the Apple II, the personal computer that launched a technology revolution and brought computers to most homes. He was inducted into the National Inventors Hall of Fame in 2000. Other computer kids are following in his footsteps.

LZAC Lossless Data Compression

Allan Chu was in fifth grade when his parents gave him a graphing calculator for his algebra class. He learned how to program it by himself and created many games for it. When he went to Johns Hopkins University's Center for Talented Youth Summer Camp, he took the calculator along. Did he become popular? "My games did," said Allan, who continued with computer inventions as a student at Saratoga High School in Saratoga, California. After being frustrated by the slow pace of downloading files from the Web, he worked on ways to shrink file sizes that were sent over the Internet. He succeeded, thus was able to send e-mails faster, and won first place in the computer science category at the 2002 Intel Science and Engineering Fair. In 2003, Allan was inducted into the National Gallery for America's Young Inventors for his work on the

LZAC Lossless Data Compression, a new algorithm that is suitable for the Internet and handheld devices. (LZAC stands for Abraham Lempel and Jacob Ziv, the fathers of dictionary-based compression, and Allan Chu.) "It achieves the best compression ratio," says Allan, who has also gained two patents for his idea. "It's simple, fast, and economical in terms of memory." ■

THE INTEL INTERNATIONAL SCIENCE AND ENGINEERING FAIR (INTEL ISEF), founded by Science Service in 1950, is the world's largest precollege celebration of science. Held annually in May, Intel ISEF brings together more than thirteen hundred finalists from approximately forty nations in a different U.S. city each year to compete in fourteen categories for over $3 million in scholarships, internships, cash prizes, and science-themed trips. The top prize is the Intel Young Scientist Award, a $50,000 college scholarship.

Think about Solving a Community Problem

Some kids take part in team programs or competitions that challenge them to find solutions to community problems. Participants do research not only by reading books but also by interviewing experts and meeting with community leaders. Sometimes they create an invention to help solve the problem, though in most cases that is not a requirement of the competition. Kids have addressed a variety of community problems.

The Dust Storm Detector

The MVCS Blazers, from Mesilla Valley Christian School in Las Cruces, New Mexico, were aware of the problems caused by dust-churning windstorms in their state. Each year motorists are injured or killed as a result of these weather systems. So team members Seth Chavez, Alex Michel, Scott Miller, and Brian Patterson worked with their team adviser, Alan Fisher, to create a working prototype warning signal that would alert drivers to dust, snow, or heavy rain. The device uses a pen laser pointer beam that is interrupted by the dust particles and activates a relay that turns on a buzzer and light. It can be used to alert the highway patrol of the location of a dust storm. They won third place in the eCYBERMISSION competition in 2003. ■

eCYBERMISSION, an online competition sponsored by the U.S. Army, asks students to use technology to solve a community problem. The army launched this competition in response to a decrease in the number of students interested in science, math, and technology careers and in recognition of the fundamental importance of these careers to the national security and the global competitiveness of the United States.

The Allergen Scanner

The Allergen Scanner is a handheld scanner that can be used by consumers to read the ingredients in products and identify whether any allergens are present. It was invented by the Scanner Patrol team from Pottstown, Pennsylvania. The team was aware that 8 percent of children and 2 percent of adults in the United States have food allergies. It's hard to tell whether these items are in common foods because they go by so many different names on the ingredients list of packaged foods. "We hope to reduce the risk that people will unknowingly ingest an allergen," said team members Jodie Leyfert, Alyse Ameer, Alexa Tietjen, and Ryan McDevitt. The students worked with a coach, science teacher Kristen Haugen. To do their research, the team members consulted sources at the Food and Drug Administration (FDA) and experts in bar code and database technologies, along with studying the labels of hundreds of food items. Then they developed their own handheld scanner system to detect eight different allergens that go by close to a hundred different names, depending on the manufacturer. The team members tested the scanner on actual product labels, and it worked. In 2004, they won the $25,000 Christopher Columbus Foundation Community Grant to develop their scanner. ■

CHRISTOPHER COLUMBUS AWARDS is a program sponsored by the Christopher Columbus Foundation in cooperation with the National Science Foundation. The program focuses on middle school students, whom it calls the Innovation Generation, and its mission is to tap their creative problem-solving potential. With the help of an adult coach, sixth- through eighth-grade students work in teams of three or four; identify a community issue; do research and consult with experts, including scientists, businesspeople, and legislators; and use science and technology to develop an innovative solution to the problem.

Avalanche Search and Survey Helicopter

Snow conditions are a continual concern in Alaska. A team of students from Alaska's East Anchorage High School proposed a solution. The students won a 2004 InvenTeams grant and worked on their design of a low-cost prototype snow robot to collect data on evolving snow conditions in high-risk, human-used areas where avalanches most often occur. ■

INVENTEAMS is a national Lemelson-MIT program. Acknowledging that most of today's inventions are created by teams, this program asks students to identify a problem that they want to address with an invention and provides them with funding to develop a prototype.

The Land Mine Protector and the Cardio-Mate

Land mines that explode unexpectedly are the cause of death and mutilation in many places around the world. In 2003, a team from Cape Henry Collegiate School in Virginia Beach, Virginia, won first place in the grades 7 through 9 category of the ExploraVision Awards for envisioning a future technology. The team's idea was for the Land Mine Protector, an unmanned dinner-plate-size aircraft that uses the Global Positioning System (GPS), a neuron-timing device, and sound waves to detect and destroy land mines without risk to human life. Another team, from Santa Rosa, California, envisioned the Cardio-Mate, a device that could be inserted in a coronary artery to detect heart failure and apply remedies, both medicinal and electronic. It could also alert health-care personnel using a miniaturized GPS. Check out the Web pages of both teams at www.exploravision. org and look under "Past Winners." ■

> EXPLORAVISION AWARDS, a competition sponsored by Toshiba and the National Science Teachers Association, which is open to students in grades K through 12 in the United States and Canada, asks entrants to study a present technology and envision its future. Its goal is to motivate students to think about their role in the future and to use creativity while applying their knowledge of science.

Think about the Needs of Others

Sometimes, if you can't think of an idea for an invention, you can focus on the needs of others, such as people close to home—a classmate, a friend, or even someone in your family.

The PaceMate

When Brandon A. Whale, of Pittsburgh, Pennsylvania, was eight years old, he was concerned about his mom, Danette Rocco, who had a pacemaker. On a regular basis, she had to send an EKG (electrocardiogram) to her doctors via the telephone. She wore special bracelets on each wrist that plugged into the phone. Electrodes in the bracelets detected her pulse. When she held a magnet up to her pacemaker, near her heart, the magnet would open up a switch in the pacemaker that allowed a transmission to be sent. Doctors could check whether the battery had power and how well her pacemaker was working.

The problem? "My mom has thin wrists," said Brandon, "and the bracelets were too big." The loose connection made it difficult for the sensors to detect her pulse. To compensate, his mom would hold her wrists against a table, pressing on the sensors.

> INVENTION CONVENTION is a general term used by many schools and school districts for an invention lesson that culminates in an invention fair.

(Left) Brandon Whale at the 1998 induction of the National Gallery for America's Young Inventors, displaying parts of his invention, the PaceMate. (Above) Brandon showing his invention to Dr. Wilson Greatbatch, the inventor of the pacemaker.

When she had to lift her hand to place the magnet up to her pacemaker, the bracelet didn't have the correct pressure. "My brother, Spencer, and I would hold the bracelet on her wrist when we were home," he said, "but what if I wasn't home? I wanted to make it easier for her." He solved the pressure problem by replacing the metal band with a hand-sewn elastic band. Then he attacked a second problem: interference. "We live in a town-house," said Brandon, "and we had to turn off our radios and TVs and ask our neighbors to turn off some of theirs to do the transmission." Through research, though, Brandon discovered that both water and electrolytes are good conductors of electricity.

So he soaked small pieces of sponges in Pedialyte, a beverage made of water and electrolytes. He placed the sponges between his mom's wrist and the bracelet, ran tests over the phone line, and checked with her doctors at the cardiac clinic about the transmissions. The improvement was marked. "After that," said Brandon, "all my mom had to do was tear open one of the Pedialyte-soaked sponges and use it when sending the transmission." Brandon called his invention the PaceMate. It was an outstanding project at the Invention Convention of his Pittsburgh elementary school. In 1998, when Brandon was inducted into the National Gallery for America's Young Inventors, Dr. Wilson Greatbatch, the inventor of the pacemaker, presented him with the award. ∎

If you still can't think of an idea for an invention, ask other people about their problems or needs. See if some aspect of their lives causes difficulties for which you can imagine a solution.

KidKare Cars

After Brandon Whale invented the PaceMate, his younger brother, Spencer, a first-grader, wanted to be an inventor, too. He was stuck for an idea, but then he thought, "Why not ask kids who are in the hospital for long periods of time, kids with cancer or other diseases, about their problems and what they'd like to see invented?" So he and his mom made arrangements to visit Children's Hospital of Pittsburgh. "While I was there, I noticed these little kids riding around in little toy cars," said Spencer. "Their moms and the nurses were running behind pushing the IV poles. When the kids would speed up, the tubes got caught in the wheels. Sometimes the parents couldn't keep up," he said. "And I realized that the kids couldn't ride the cars if the nurses weren't available or their parents weren't there."

Spencer's idea? To make a toy car with an IV pole attached. First, he wanted to build a prototype, but unfortunately, he didn't have a toy car, an IV pole, or the money to buy them. He decided to enter only the idea for what he called "KidKare ride toys" into a monthly contest called Student Ideas for a Better America, which awards a $100 prize. He won! Although he was ready to spend his own money on buying a toy car, he received a nice surprise. The owner of Step 2 Ride Equipment in Streetsboro, Ohio, had read a newspaper article about Spencer's plan and pitched in by donating toy cars and a wagon.

The project was under way. Children's Hospital of Pittsburgh donated broken IV poles. Then, Spencer's grandmother got into the act. She worked at Duquesne Light Company, where several mechanics donated their free time to weld the IV poles onto the toy cars. Spencer decorated the IV poles with colored tape. The cars are now used at the Children's Hospital in Pittsburgh.

Winthrop-University Hospital in Mineola, New York, heard of the project and wanted some KidKare ride toys, too. The hospital invited Spencer to visit and arranged for six cars to be constructed as an Eagle Scout project under Spencer's supervision. "How cool is that?" said Maxine Andrade of the Cancer Center for Kids at the hospital. "Children are still children, even on chemotherapy. Parents have told me how much they appreciate these cars." In 2000, Spencer, at age eight, was inducted into the National Gallery for America's Young Inventors. ■

Inventor's Tip

"If you have an idea, stay with it, no matter how dumb you think it sounds. If it solves a problem and helps you, chances are it will do the same for any number of people."

—*Austin Meggitt, 1999 inductee into the National Gallery for America's Young Inventors for the Glove and Battie Caddie*

STUDENT IDEAS FOR A BETTER AMERICA is a monthly contest open to students (grades K through 8 and 9 through 12) sponsored by the Partnership for America's Future, a nonprofit organization that also sponsors the National Gallery for America's Young Inventors. Students are asked to think only of an idea, not to create a model, for a new product or an improvement on an existing product. The goal is to encourage the learning, insight, creativity, and workmanship of America's students and to demonstrate that valuable ideas can be created by America's youths.

Find an Idea through Research

Sometimes you can find the solution for a problem almost by accident. In 1970, Stephanie Kwolek, a research scientist at Du Pont, was experimenting with polymers when she created one that a technician was hesitant to spin into a fiber for fear it would clog the spinneret. Stephanie had her doubts as well but reviewed her work and convinced the technician to try. The spun fiber is now known as Kevlar. It is lightweight yet five times stronger than steel and is used to make airplanes, skis, bulletproof vests, and many other things.

You might be doing research on a subject when you read about a problem you think you can solve. Keep researching and start experimenting, and you may just have your invention.

The Microelectrochemical Sensor and Plating System

Elina Onitskansky read an article about the economic difficulties that corporations face in trying to meet Environmental Protection Agency (EPA) standards regarding water pollution and the adverse effects it has on the environment. Elina, a student at Hathaway Brown School in Shaker Heights, Ohio, felt inspired to do something about it. Currently, the cost of water cleanup is huge, and detection involves complex technology that can't be run continuously. As part of her school's research program, Elina worked with mentor Dr. Chung Chiun Liu and other scientists in a lab at Case Western Reserve University, which specializes in sensor technology. She used the lab facilities to create her own sensor. It is about three-quarters of an inch in size, costs about $25, and will simultaneously detect six of the most common metallic ion water pollutants in real time. Then, her electroplating system will remove the offensive metals from the water, cleaning it up! She hopes that her sensors will be used in streams and pipes that lead away from factories. She was a semifinalist at the Siemens Westinghouse Competition in Math, Science & Technology and a 2001 inductee into the National Gallery for America's Young Inventors. ■

> THE SIEMENS WESTINGHOUSE COMPETITION IN MATH, SCIENCE & TECHNOLOGY is open to high school students, either as individuals or in teams of two or three. Regional winners advance to the national competition in Washington, D.C. The competition is administered by the College Board and funded by the Siemens Foundation.

Biodegradable Disposable Diaper

When fourteen-year-old Rishi Vasudeva was trying to think of a science fair project for his ninth-grade biology class at Roswell High School in Roswell, Georgia, he happened to watch a diaper commercial on television. "I jokingly chose

Rishi Vasudeva with his display for a biodegradable disposable diaper.

diapers as my topic," said Rishi. Once he discovered that the water-repellent outer lining of disposable diapers takes more than four hundred years to degrade, he grew concerned. Billions of them are dumped yearly into landfills around the country. "My interest moved quickly away from it being simply a joke," he said. He spent the next four years developing a better diaper. An internship at the Department of Agriculture was part of his studies. He eventually started working with zein, a protein made from corn that is currently used as a coating for pills. He was able to create a film out of zein and other materials to serve as an outer lining for diapers. His zein-lined diaper degrades in about thirty days and is seven times cooler than others on the shelves. Rishi was a regional finalist in the Siemens Westinghouse Competition in Math, Science & Technology in 2000. In 2001, Rishi was inducted into the National Gallery for America's Young Inventors and was a finalist in the Intel Science Talent Search. ■

THE INTEL SCIENCE TALENT SEARCH (STS), often called the "junior Nobel Prize," was created in 1942. Each year, forty finalists (taken from three hundred semifinalists and more than fifteen hundred applicants) come to Washington, D.C., to participate in the Science Talent Institute. There they present their work to the media and the general public at the National Academy of Sciences and are judged on their scientific knowledge as they compete for the top prize—a $100,000 college scholarship.

The Effect of Neem Oil on Mosquitoes

Peter Borden was living in Fort Myers, Florida, where mosquitoes are a public health threat. "I like going outside," said Peter, "and in Florida in the summer, especially at night, you can get eaten alive." The seventh-grader at Canterbury School decided to research the topic of mosquitoes and discovered that the insecticide cities used to control them is very toxic. Peter wanted to find a safer alternative and under the guidance of his science teacher, Dr. Betsy Glass, arranged to conduct experiments in a county mosquito lab. He started experimenting with the oil of the neem tree, a biodegradable, environmentally friendly substance used to kill some insects, including mosquitoes. "He discovered the proper concentration of neem oil to place in a water-filled beaker that could be used to kill all the mosquitoes," said Glass, "but not be harmful to humans or other beneficial organisms." Peter was a 2003 finalist in the Discovery Channel Young Scientist Challenge. ■

> THE DISCOVERY CHANNEL YOUNG SCIENTIST CHALLENGE was launched by Discovery Communications, Inc., in partnership with Science Service, to nurture the next generation of American scientists at a critical age when interest in science begins to decline. More than sixty thousand middle school students from around the country enter science projects in one of the science and engineering fairs affiliated with Science Service; then, six thousand of them are nominated by their fair directors to enter their projects in the Discovery Channel Young Scientist Challenge, a program that does not require but sometimes results in inventions.

Find a Use for Something You Discover

As you work on a project, you may discover things or come to realizations that surprise you. In 1968, Dr. Spencer Silver, a scientist at the 3M Company, was trying to develop a strong adhesive but created a weak one instead. He added it to paper, but since it wasn't very strong, he didn't think much about it. He shared some of the paper with his friend, Art Fry, who used the paper to mark the pages in his hymnal while singing in the church choir. He liked that the paper could easily stick on, then peel off again—and that's how the Post-it was invented.

Knowing what to do with a discovery is an important part of the inventing process. A talented inventor will see possibilities that others don't. One young inventor made a discovery, then was prompted to find a use for it—an invention.

Fenugreek-Treated Paper

Kavita Shukla, of Maryland, was in middle school when she started her research on fenugreek, an Indian herb used to spice food.

It was on trips to India to visit her grandparents that she first learned about the spice from her grandmother, who gave Kavita a drink of water mixed with a bit of fenugreek powder after Kavita drank some tap water. "The tap water in India is often contaminated with bacteria," said Kavita. "When I didn't get sick, I became curious."

After returning home, she began to do some experiments on fenugreek, which began quite simply and became more complicated as she continued her research in high school. Kavita's first step was to gather samples of polluted water from her backyard and from bacteria-infested ponds. In the kitchen, she added various concentrations of gold-colored fenugreek powder. When Kavita checked on the water samples, they didn't look like water mixed with fenugreek powder. Instead, the fenugreek powder formed clumps in the water. To remove the bacteria and the fenugreek, she could just scoop out the clump.

"It was very impressive," said Kavita. Then she accidentally left one of the pond water samples alone for a few weeks. The next time she looked at it, she saw that the bacteria had not grown in the sample. It happened to be the sample that contained fenugreek powder. "That's what gave me the idea to start doing bacterial and fungal growth experiments," said Kavita.

Then, one day her mom came home from shopping with a package of strawberries. "Most of the strawberries were rotten," said Kavita, who then wondered whether fenugreek mixed with water could be sprayed on strawberries at the farm or once they were packaged. Would that inhibit bacterial or fungal growth and keep them fresh?

She mixed water and fenugreek, put it in a spray bottle, and sprayed the mixture on the good strawberries. "The spray was very effective. It slowed down the rotting process," she said, "and the strawberries tasted better." Next, Kavita wondered if fenugreek could be used as a packaging material for food. She needed to prove her idea, so she set up three experiments with paper towels. First, she soaked a paper towel with a mixture of fenugreek and water, let it dry, and set some strawberries on it. Then, she soaked another paper towel in detergent mixed with water, let it dry, and set strawberries on it as well. Finally, to see the

Kavita Shukla, the inventor of Fenugreek-Treated Paper, in the lab.

difference between what would happen with the treated paper towel and the nontreated paper towel, she set out an ordinary paper towel and put strawberries on it.

Kavita waited and observed. Her fenugreek-treated paper towel kept the strawberries fresh much longer than the other paper towels did. What a discovery! A natural, non-toxic, biodegradable way to preserve food.

"It was very simple, and that's why it is so useful," said Kavita. "It can be used very easily in third-world countries." She was granted a patent for her fenugreek-treated paper in the spring of 2002. Several companies have approached her about using her process. "I want to make sure," she added, "that it's able to reach all the people who would benefit from this invention, especially those in third-world countries." In 2001, she was inducted into the National Gallery for America's Young Inventors. She has won numerous awards and was also the recipient of the Lemelson-MIT High School Invention Apprenticeship in 2002. ∎

Is Your Idea an Invention?

You think you have a great idea for an invention. Okay, you've got one more step: find out whether anyone else has thought of the idea. Ask your family and your classmates whether they've ever heard of or seen a product like your invention. Ask your neighbors. Visit a store that handles products similar to yours, and inspect the shelves for anything that resembles your idea. Ask clerks whether they know of any products like yours. Find magazines or catalogues with ads showing products in the same category as your idea (that is, toy, sport, kitchen, or household magazines). Then check the Internet. Use a search engine such as Google and type in search words that describe your idea for an invention. Lots of stores, supply houses, catalogues, and magazines have Web sites that feature products. What were the results of your search?

If you haven't found anything like your product on the market, great! If you find something similar, don't get discouraged. Many inventions are very much like another invention except for a small change. That's what *new* means. Examine the product. Think about how your idea is different and how you can improve on the existing product.

Inventor's Tip

"The biggest thing is to find a good problem. For a contest, you want something that everybody can relate to, so that right when they see it, they say, 'That's a great idea.'"

—*Charles Johnson, national champion, 1996 Invent America! Student Invention Contest for the Train Detecting Device*

Activities

1. Brainstorm Ideas for Inventions

   Brainstorming means to engage in organized shared problem solving. Many inventors, old and young, brainstorm to think of ideas. No criticism is allowed. Crazy ideas are encouraged. To get started, pick a subject, then throw out any ideas you have about it. For example,

- Think of all the things you do every day or on holidays or weekends. Then, think about any problems, things that bug you about doing them, or ways to make them better.

- Think about all the tools or utensils you use in an ordinary day—fork, knife, toothbrush, shovel, broom, scissors, and so on. What would make them easier to use? Or better?

- Go from room to room in your house. Brainstorm ideas as you look at items in the kitchen, the bathroom, the den, the bedroom, and so on. Could you use an ordinary item for a new purpose? Or make it out of a different material?

- Combine two or more existing objects to create a new one—for example, a fork and a spoon.

- Pick any invention that you have in your home or classroom. Envision an improvement for it twenty years in the future. (Note: If you like this activity, you might be interested in the ExploraVision Competition. Check out www.exploravision.com for more information.)

2. Do a Survey

Inventing with a specific person or need in mind is often a good idea. Ask others what they need. Even if another person thinks of the idea, the real problem is making a model of the idea and proving that it can work. That's your job. Use the following questions to start. Then, add your own questions to the survey.

Chores

    a. Which household activities do you hate to do?

    b. What is it about them that you don't like?

    c. What would make them easier?

Sports

    a. What is your favorite leisure activity or sport?

    b. Do you have any problems in doing the activity? For example, are you too hot or too cold, do you fall down or run into things?

    c. What would make the activity easier, safer, or more fun?

There are lots of other categories to do surveys about. Make up a survey about an area that interests you.

3. List Some Problems and Solutions

Chores: Kids and adults have to do chores around the house or in the yard. List some of your chores and the problems that come up when you do them. Can you think of ways to make these chores easier?

Common Chores	What problems come up in doing these chores?	What would make the chores easier to do?	Any invention ideas?

People's Needs: Think about people and their needs when looking for ideas. Use this table to list some problems experienced by different types of people.

Kinds of people	What problems do they face?	What would help them with these problems?	Any invention ideas?
Babies			
Toddlers			
Kids who play sports			
Physically impaired people			
Older people			

A Better World: How can you help make the world a better place with an invention? Use this table to list problems experienced all over the world, and think about ways to solve them.

Issue	What are the problems?	What would make the situation better?	Any invention ideas?
Environment			
Safety			
Natural disasters			

Keeping a Journal or an Inventor's Log and Writing a Report

Do you remember all of your ideas for inventions, even the really wacky ones? Or all the problems you think of that could be solved by an invention? It's easy to forget a few details. That's why inventors write notes in a log or a journal. Journal entries or log notes are part of the invention process. They are a record of your work and are proof of what you did. Thomas Edison, who gained Patent No. 223,898 for his Electric Lamp, was twenty-one when he gained the first of his 1,093 patents. It was for an electrical vote recorder. He filled thirty-four hundred notebooks, his inventor's log, with ideas and details of his experiments.

Edison summarized his work on his patent applications. Many young inventors summarize their work in reports, and like Edison, they consult their journal or log for details.

Logs and Journals

Logs or journals are like diaries. Write about your ideas, your guesses, and your successes and failures. List questions that occur to you. Keep a record of problems that you need to solve and write down ideas that come to you while brainstorming. As you prepare to build a model of your invention, list the materials that you buy and save your store receipts. Don't forget to list the steps you take to construct your model. When anything goes wrong, be sure to write that down as well. Then, describe how you solve each problem.

Keep a record of the names of people you talk to, what you talked about, and how they helped you. For example, if you consult with people who know a lot about products like yours, people who might know whether your idea is an invention, jot down their comments. Make note of the equipment you use and whether you use it by yourself or with the help of others. Record the information you gathered from researching in books or on the Internet, including the book titles and the Internet addresses. For books, list the title, the author, the publisher, and the year of publication, as well as the pages where you come upon useful information. For information found on the Internet, list the name of the Web site, the title of the page you are referencing, and the full Internet address. Getting help from books, the Internet, or other people is a good practice, but it's important to clarify what you learned from different sources.

Just be yourself as you write in your log or journal. Your entries can reflect your personality. Every inventor has a unique way of jotting down ideas or making sketches. You can also include pictures of your invention in progress and of yourself working on it.

Log or journal pages should include a place for witnesses' signatures. A signature by a witness is proof that someone reviewed your progress by looking at your model, observing your experiments, or reading your journal. It provides proof that you completed a certain amount of work by a particular date. At the end of the section that the witness reads, you can create a signature line, with a place for the date. Then, ask your witness to sign and date it. Different people can witness your work, such as teachers, advisers, or mentors. Parents do not usually witness journals or logs, since they are often working with you. You might want to have someone witness your work every day, once a week, or once a month, depending on how long you work on the project and on the requirements of any contests you intend to enter.

Inventor's Tip

"Write in the journal every time you work on your invention or think of ideas. Important stuff to include would be something like where you looked to see if your idea had been invented already. Something that is not important is what else you did that day, like that you went to the movies after you worked on your invention."

—*Luke Bader, Meritorious Award winner, Invent Iowa 2003 State Invention Convention for the Walk Along*

The standard inventor's log or journal is a bound composition book that is available at most office supply stores. The pages are sewn in so that it's clear if one has been torn out. Some composition books come with numbered pages. A missing number would also indicate a missing page. Why is that important? A log or a journal is for notes, mistakes and all. Nothing should be torn out or covered over with correction fluid. This applies only to students who write their notes by hand. Today, many kid inventors write their notes on computers. Whatever the form, your log should contain all of your ideas, steps, and experiments—including your mistakes.

If you are inventing for a class assignment or a competition, you should create whatever type of log or journal is required by your teacher or by the competition rules. The requirements vary from program to program. For example:

The Inventive Thinking Curriculum Project, an outreach program of the United States Patent and Trademark Office, includes these Rules for Authentic Journal Keeping:

- Using a bound notebook, make notes each day about what you do and learn while working on your invention.
- Record your idea and how you got it.
- Write about problems you have and how you solve them.
- Write in ink and do not erase.
- Add sketches and drawings to make things clear.
- List all parts, sources, and costs of materials.
- Sign and date all entries at the time they are made and have them witnessed.

The Craftsman/NSTA Young Inventors Award Program challenges students to invent a tool and includes the following guidelines for entries:

- Must be typed and double spaced on 8½-by-11-inch white paper.
- Text color should be black, and no type should be smaller than 12-point.
- Log, including a photo page, should be no less than three pages and no longer than eight pages.
- Stapled in the upper left-hand corner.

Students must also answer the following questions:

- How does your tool work?
- Who helped you build your tool?
- What safety procedures should you keep in mind when using your tool invention?
- What were the sequential steps you took to build your tool?
- What problems did you encounter?
- How did you solve these problems?
- What hand tools did you use?
- How would you improve your tool?

The New Hampshire Young Inventors Program (YIP) suggests many guidelines for inventor's logs, including:

- Write in ink and do not erase.
- Leave no empty spaces.
- Use a bound notebook.
- Make a diagram of your ideas whenever possible.
- Describe all of the materials and parts you use. List your costs.
- Sign and date all entries at the time they are made and have them witnessed at least once a week.

Inventor's Tip

"My log consists of pictures of circuit board development and of the project developing and describes the project being conducted in great detail. The log ended up being about a hundred pages long by the conclusion."

—Ryan Patterson, inventor of the American Sign Language Translator; first place, 2001 Siemens Westinghouse Competition in Math, Science & Technology; winner, 2002 Intel Science Talent Search; winner, 2002 Glenn Seaborg Award (which included a trip to the Nobel Prize Awards)

Examples of student log and journal entries follow. Your own entries and reports will be unique because they will be about your project and will reflect your interests, but you can get some ideas from other young inventors.

The Waterbike

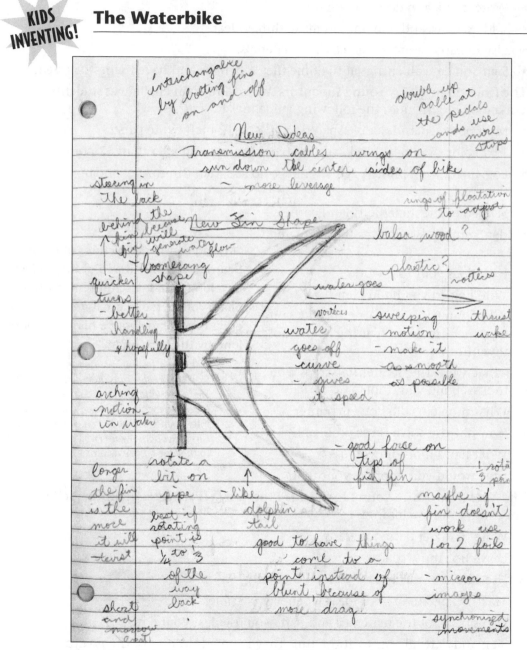

A page from Krysta Morlan's log showing a sketch and notes about a part of her Waterbike.

Krysta Morlan, like many inventors, started by imagining how her invention would look. She drew sketches of her ideas in her log, then made notes about them. Sketching can be an easy way to portray ideas that are hard to express in words alone. Take a close look at the page from Krysta's log. She drew a fish tail that would be the back wheel of her waterbike. Her handwritten notes include

---

New Ideas

- Like dolphin fin
- Water goes off curve—gives it speed
- Good force on tips of fish fin

Her notes are simple, yet they reveal her ideas and how these led to her final invention.

Krysta lived in the town of Vacaville, California, where it gets very hot in the summer. Due to a series of surgeries she had when she was in tenth grade, she had been in hip-to-ankle casts for more than a year. The casts were very uncomfortable, so Krysta invented the Cast Cooler, a battery-powered device to ventilate her casts. It won an award in a national contest sponsored by Duracell (the contest no longer exists, but it asked students to create battery-powered inventions). Later, Krysta was selected as the winner of the first annual Invention Apprenticeship for high school students, sponsored by the Lemelson-MIT Program. For her apprenticeship, Krysta worked with Colin Twitchell, the director of the Lemelson Assistive Technology Development Center in Amherst, Massachusetts, to develop her next invention. In thinking about what to invent, Krysta remembered that when she'd had the casts on, she couldn't do her favorite activities—biking and swimming—but she could do water exercises to retrain and strengthen her legs. She also remembered how bored she was doing those exercises, so she came up with the idea for a waterbike. It would be made of PVC pipe and foam, enabling it to float, and would have a rudder for steering. (PVC stands for polyvinyl chloride, and it is the plastic from which pipes are made.) When she built it, instead of a back wheel, she built a fin like the one she had sketched in her log. As she pedaled, the fin moved from side to side to propel the bike through the water. She named her invention the Waterbike. In 2000, Krysta was listed in *ID* magazine as one of the "Fresh Forty" designers under age thirty. ■

The Walk Along

Luke Bader, a fourth-grader from St. Athanasius School in Jesup, Iowa, called his log a journal. As part of the requirements called for by Invent Iowa, an annual statewide program, he wrote all of his journal entries by hand as he worked, then later typed out his notes on 8½-by-11-inch white paper. He also had his journal witnessed by an adult.

Luke's younger brother Joe suffers from a chromosomal disorder that affects him both physically and mentally. Luke's family had tried several devices to assist Joe with walking. "None of the things they used helped Joe walk," said Luke. "He'd sit in them, but nothing moved his legs or was attached to them. All those things were costing a lot of money, so I decided to make something for a lot less money." His mom and dad helped him with the project. "It was just kind of a three-way deal," said his dad, Lee Bader. "I helped him drill holes. We brainstormed."

Luke's first journal entry was

> January 11, 2003
> Decided on basic idea for project. The problem was that my little brother can't walk, and he's at the age where he should be walking. I want to help him. I decided to make the Walk Along. How it works:
>
> 1. Attach the small ends of the Walk Along to the child.
>
> 2. Attach the other ends to your legs.
>
> 3. You walk and the other person's legs move along with yours.

Luke's journal also describes his dad's involvement and lists other people he talked to and the advice he got from them.

> January 25, 2003
> My dad and I cut the PVC pipe, and we drilled one hole to use to keep the pipes together. I cut the plastic lemonade containers for the ends to put around the legs. I also put on the Velcro strips.
>
> We met Joe's physical therapist, Barb Kaufman, from Early Developmental Intervention at Covenant Medical Center in Waterloo. I showed her Joe's Walk Along as much as it was complete. She gave me some moleskin to make it more comfortable. She gave me suggestions on how long to make it. We tried it out with Joe.

After testing the Walk Along, Luke recorded the results.

> January 29, 2003
> I went with Joseph to his school. We tried the Walk Along. Joe's aide, Diana, and his teacher, Leanna, and Joe's other physical therapist, Cindy Brown, watched. I think it went well, until Joe got tired.

Luke included some additional advice he got from the physical therapist that led to an improvement of his design.

February 3, 2003
Barb Kaufman gave us a plastic strap for in-between the Walk-Along. It worked better when we added it.

He also listed his materials and what they cost.

List of materials for the Walk Along

1. Velcro and foam donated by Clark and Associates
2. Moleskin and plastic strip donated by Early Developmental Intervention
3. PVC pipes $2.10
4. PVC fittings   .94
5. Bolts and nuts   .08
6. Plastic from lemonade containers   .00

                                    TOTAL $3.12

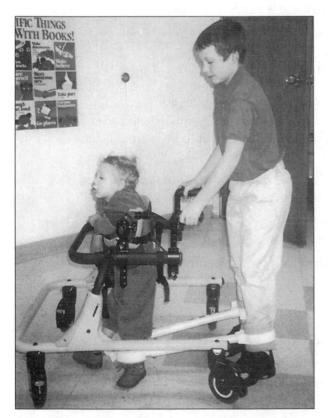

Joe has been using the Walk Along. "One time I actually saw him moving his feet forward," said Luke. And now Luke is making another one for someone else to try. He won his school competition and also won a Meritorious Award at the statewide Invent Iowa 2003 State Invention Convention for the Walk Along.

Luke's family was very proud of him. "When the project was completed, we took a picture of Luke and Joe using the Walk Along," his mom said. "It all came together. It was more than Luke realized. It was a pretty neat thing to do." His dad agreed, saying, "It's probably one of the greatest things that has ever happened to us. Who would have believed that something that started as a school project would be able to help his brother?" ■

Luke Bader helping his brother Joe use his invention, the Walk Along.

The Gumball Machine

KIDS INVENTING!

Outside Lindsey Clement's house in Longview, Texas, there are fifteen sweet gum trees. Hundreds of walnut-size spiky pods ("gumballs") fall off the trees and have to be cleaned up. "I couldn't do it all in one day," said Lindsey. "I'd go out every day for about thirty minutes or an hour, pick them up with my bare hands, and put them in a bucket. I didn't like it too much." That motivated her to create the Gumball Machine. After Lindsey gained an honorable mention at her school invention fair, her teacher suggested that she also enter the Craftsman/NSTA Young Inventors Awards Program.

To answer the question How does your tool work? Lindsey wrote in her inventor's log:

> To work my invention, you simply push the machine (like a lawnmower) over the sweet gumballs in the yard. The wire mesh wheels pick up the spiney balls. As the wheels turn, they push the sweet gumballs forward until they hit a smooth, narrow block of wood that makes them fall into a bag that is attached to the machine. The machine is light enough in weight that it is easy to lift.

In answer to other specific contest questions, Lindsey wrote in her log:

> **Who helped you build your tool?**
> My dad helped me with this project from start to finish.
>
> **What were the sequential steps you took to build your tool?**
> The first task we faced was to find a way to make the gumballs cling to the wheels as they rolled over the gumballs. This turned out to be more difficult than we imagined.
>
> * We first used Styrofoam wheels, but the gumballs would not stick to the Styrofoam. Back to the drawing board.
>
> * We then tried some wooden wheels that my dad sanded down to a point. We spaced them just slight enough to allow a gumball to go between them.
>
> * When this did not work so well, we took some nylon hose and stretched it over the wheels. The machine picked up a few balls, but it was still not as effective as we thought it should be.
>
> Again, back to the drawing board.

Lindsey wrote a very clear description of the steps she and her dad took and the problems they encountered, including the different things they tried and the results—failures as well as successes.

Lindsey Clement with the Gumball Machine.

At that point in the project, Lindsey's dad had about given up. He didn't think they'd find a material that would pick up the gumballs. Then one day while Lindsey was in her dad's workshop, she spied a roll of wire mesh. It was hard but flexible. Just the material I need, Lindsey thought. She and her dad laid a Frisbee on top of the wire mesh and used it as a pattern to cut wire wheels. "My dad stressed safety so I wore gloves when we were cutting the wire mesh because the ends can get a little sharp," said Lindsey.

Lindsey continued to answer the contest questions in her log:

How did you solve the problems you encountered?

- We spaced the eight wire wheels about 1 inch apart with smaller wooden pieces in between. We put it on an axle made of PVC pipe. Bingo! It picked up the sweet gumballs.

- Next, we had to find a way to make the sweet gumballs drop over into a basket. We attached some fingerlike prongs to the axle and in between the wheels. We made the prongs of some thin Plexiglas. It was too brittle and broke easily.

- Then, we tried some small wooden pieces that we sanded smooth to allow the ball to roll right off. We attached each piece to the axle in between the wheels. Yes! It would work, except we were losing several balls off the sides of the machine. So we built some guards on either side out of Plexiglas to help guide the balls forward.

- Finally, all we lacked was a handle and a basket to catch the balls. We built both the handle frame and the basket frame out of PVC pipe and PVC connectors. My dad and I sewed a cloth basket to attach to the frame. Now we were in business.

Lindsey's answers show that she and her dad talked about how to solve a series of problems. They tried one solution, then another. It's obvious how well they worked together. Her log clearly lists all the steps that went into creating her invention, and her comments show that she was thinking and solving problems throughout the project. That's what judges like to see. Lindsey was a national winner in the second- through fifth-grade category in the Craftsman/NSTA Young Inventors Award Program for her Gumball Machine. She was an inductee into the National Gallery for America's Young Inventors in 2001. ■

KIDS INVENTING! The Glove and Battie Caddie

Austin Meggitt was a fourth-grader from Shupe Middle School in Amherst, Ohio, when he used the Invent America! log to record the steps of his invention process. Unlike Invent Iowa or the Craftsman/NSTA Young Inventors Award Program, the Invent America! Student Invention Contest provides a log form. On the one used by Austin, the left side of the page has a column with lines for written notes. On the right side is a blank area—a place for sketches, photos, and copies of receipts.

In his log, Austin wrote lots of daily entries about his ideas and his trips to the store. He also included photos of himself sawing, measuring, and drilling while he made his invention, the Glove and Battie Caddie. It's a device to carry a baseball bat and a mitt on a bike. "I thought of 'caddie' because it carries things," said Austin. "Then I just changed 'bat' to 'battie' to rhyme with 'caddie.'"

As he began his project, he wrote,

> Wednesday, 11/12/97
> Today I talked with Dale from Dale's Bike Shop. He said he has been in the bike business for fourteen years. He was checking for me whether my invention was new. Every month he gets sent a CD that lists parts and accessories for bikes. This month's had 127,679 parts. My invention was not listed. I felt very excited because I began to think that perhaps one day my Bike Clamp would be in the list of 127,680 parts and accessories.

Judges who read this entry would know one of the steps Austin took to discover whether his idea was something new, an invention. Austin also included notes about gathering materials and about his father's participation in the project—important information that any log should contain.

> Saturday, 11/15/97
> Today I went to Lowe's in search of materials for my invention. My dad and I brainstormed while walking through the aisles. We examined different

(continued)

clamping devices until we narrowed it down to a couple of possible choices. Next, we searched for something that would serve as a base for the device. We chose ½-inch PVC pipe. My dad challenged me to figure out how I was to connect the bracket to the handlebars. I came up with a few good ideas, and with my dad's help I was able to come up with what seemed like a workable solution.

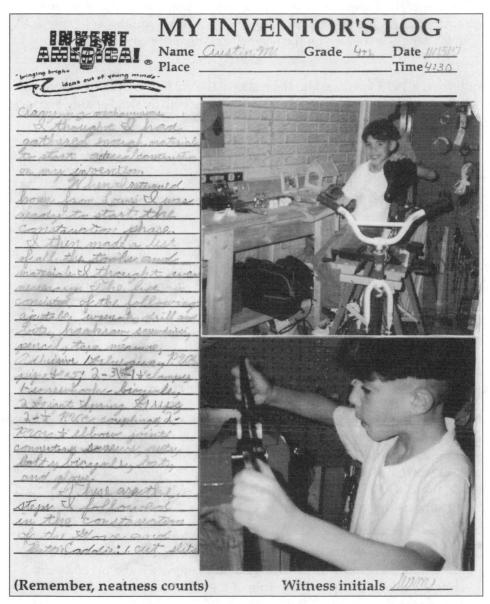

A page from Austin Meggitt's Invention Log for the Invent America! Student Invention Contest.

Austin also wrote a report about his work and added a series of pictures about the story of his invention—from start to finish, complete with cartoon captions. He showed himself riding on a bike while trying to hold onto the handlebars and his glove and bat. The caption read: "This is really dangerous." Another photo shows him riding the bike after he'd installed the Glove and Battie Caddie on it. In his report, he wrote the following description of the purpose of his device.

> The use of the Glove and Battie Caddie allows the rider to maintain proper control of a bicycle by eliminating the need to hang onto his equipment. A rider's hands can remain on the handlebars where they should be.

Austin was a 1999 inductee into the National Gallery for America's Young Inventors. His invention is sold in stores, through an arrangement with By Kids For Kids, and is called the Battie Caddie. ■

Reports

Reports are different from logs or journals. A report is a summary of your project and a description of your finished invention. Reports can also include sketches, charts, graphs, or photographs.

Some programs ask students to submit reports, rather than journals or logs. Others require students to create Web sites to record their results. The Christopher Columbus Awards Program requests that students submit a report that covers four topics: the Issue, Research, Testing, and the Solution. In their work, students must address a community problem. Some of the student solutions are inventions, although that is not a requirement.

Pressure Blowout Smoke Diverter

One team from Hatfield, Pennsylvania, that entered the Christopher Columbus Awards Program wrote its report about creating a prototype of a Pressure Blowout Smoke Diverter. Team members Steven Levandusky, Daniel Pearson, and Eric Seagreaves worked with coach Joan Hurd to develop the project, and they were semi-finalists in the 2001 Christopher Columbus Awards Program. Their report included the following answers to the program's topics:

> *The Issue*: Smoke inhalation is a frequent cause of death or serious injury in house fires, particularly those that occur at night, when the occupants of a home are usually asleep and unaware of the life-threatening situation.
>
> *(continued)*

Research: Using newspapers, a book (*The Essentials of Firefighting*, 4th ed.), a video (*Fire Power*, produced by the National Fire Protection Association), and the Internet, the team learned about the devastating effects of smoke inhalation and the ways it can be avoided. The students' research led them to the concept of positive-pressure ventilation, and from that concept, the team developed an idea for a ventilation system that could push smoke out of a room and bring in fresh air in the event of a fire. Before building a prototype, the team consulted with a fire training coordinator from the county fire academy and a safety engineer, both of whom supported the idea.

Testing: The team built a small model house out of Plexiglas. The house consisted of two rooms with a hallway between them. Each room had a window and a door. In the window of one of the rooms, the team installed a fan, which could be activated by a smoke detector, located in the hallway. Burning incense, also located in the hallway, was used as a smoke source. During several trials, with the rooms' doors and windows opened and closed in different combinations, the fan reacted to the smoke detector and increased the air pressure in the room. Because the air pressure in the room was greater than that in the hallway, the smoke could not enter the room with the fan. Instead, it escaped into the room without the fan.

The Solution: Many lives could be saved by the use of a window fan, designed to activate at the earliest detection of smoke, that employs positive-pressure ventilation to divert smoke out and pump fresh air in to a room In a burning building. The team's goal was to patent, manufacture, and market such a device to building contractors and the general public.

The Hatfield, Pennsylvania, team members' report describes their invention and summarizes the problem, their research and tests, and their solution, without listing any of their daily activities. Yet if you read between the lines, you know that they kept careful notes about the daily activities of their project in logs or journals as they worked. ■

Inventor's Logs, Journals, and Reports as Part of a Display

After you finish your invention, the next step may be entering it in an invention fair at your school. You'll get a chance to display your invention and talk about it. A student log or journal is part of each entry. Often, in your display you must include reports that summarize all your work. Usually, you will arrange these paper records on a table next to the model of your invention and in front of a display board that explains the project.

At an invention fair, judges read your log, journal, or report to understand how you did the work, find out who helped you and what equipment you used, and learn about problems you encountered and how you solved them. If a project is very complicated, a judge will want to know what you did yourself, what was done by others, and what advice or knowledge you received from others. A log, a journal, or a report should be able to answer many of the judges' questions.

Inventor's Tip

"Always keep a journal because they are a great way to keep track of your thoughts. When you are brainstorming for ideas, always write them down because you will want to come back to them later. Also, be sure to keep it dated. No matter how smart you think you are, you'll probably forget some details. It also helps to just have things down on paper to look at, and also to act as hard evidence that you thought of an idea and to map out your thinking process."

—*Austin Meggitt, 1999 inductee into the National Gallery for America's Young Inventors for the Glove and Battie Caddie*

Activities

1. Test Your Descriptive Abilities.

   • Describe an invention that you use all the time, such as a fork, a broom, a toaster, a weed whacker, or a scooter. Show your description to a friend and see if he or she can identify the item based on your description.

   • After reading the directions for operating a toy or a piece of equipment or playing a game, write step-by-step directions in your own words. Then ask your friends to use these directions to play with the toy or the game or use the equipment.

   • Write directions for how to use your own invention.

2. Sketch a Favorite Invention or Your Own Invention.

   • Make a sketch or a drawing of an invention or of your idea for an invention in your log or journal. It can be either a simple sketch or a complicated one. Label each part of the invention. Use notes to explain each part and how the parts interact. Try to sketch the front view, the back view, a side view, and the top view.

   • Do a patent drawing. For examples of the style of patent drawings required by the U.S. Patent and Trademark Office, check out *How to Make Patent Drawings Yourself* by Jack Lo and David Pressman (Nolo Press, 2003). Look at the examples and try to do the same kind of drawings, either by hand or on a computer.

3

Making a Model

Amodel is the proof that an invention idea can actually work. Maybe you dream about finding a way for people to fly without airplanes or about a car that runs without gasoline, but can your idea become a reality? Wilbur and Orville Wright weren't the only people who had an idea for an airplane, but until the Wright brothers took flight, the airplane was just a great idea. They gained Patent No. 821,393 for their Flying Machine in 1906.

Think about all the ideas for inventions that you've listed in your log or journal. Which of these could you actually make?

Making a model can involve plenty of trial and error. Sometimes inventors are successful as they work, but often they aren't. Failure is part of the invention process, and so is change. You may need to try one thing, then another, in making a working model of your idea. Thomas Edison once said that genius is 1 percent inspiration and 99 percent perspiration. To find the right filament for his lightbulb, he tested thousands of materials. As Edison did, you'll need to evaluate all of your results and solve problems as you work. For example, you may find that certain materials are not strong enough or flexible enough or don't have some other needed quality. If that's the case, you'll just have to try other materials.

Sometimes accidents are part of the invention process. In the 1950s, Patsy Sherman and Sam Smith were working at 3M trying to invent a new

Inventor's Tip

"Most of my invention ideas were for things I thought would be cool to have. For example, a hover car or a guitar with an automated tuner. I would discuss my ideas with my mom, and we would end up revising the ideas to things I could actually make."

—Mitchell Weiss, inventor of the Pedal Powered Lawn Mower; national finalist, 2001 Craftsman/NSTA Young Inventors Awards Program type of synthetic rubber that could be used to make fuel lines for jet engines. When some of the material accidentally dropped onto a technician's shoe, it coated that part of the shoe. Nothing Patsy and Sam tried—soapy water, acetone, or any other solvent—would remove it or even make the area wet. The polymer material made a great fabric protector. Yet it took seven years of experiments before Patsy and Sam created the first successful molecule that led to the popular 3M product called Scotchgard.

Inventor's Tip

"When I come up with an idea, I usually find a Web site that shows how hobbyists did a similar thing. A lot of basic projects have already been done and documented. It's good to use the Net to find some specific background information on the project you're thinking about doing."

—Ryan Patterson, inventor of the American Sign Language Translator; first place, 2001 Siemens Westinghouse Competition in Math, Science & Technology; winner, 2002 Intel Science Talent Search; winner, 2002 Glenn Seaborg Award (which included a trip to the Nobel Prize Awards)

Oftentimes, making a model can also help you develop an idea. You start out with one idea, but as you work on the model, both the model and the idea change.

The Matrix Wheelchair Seat

When she was fourteen and a freshman at Bartlesville High School in Bartlesville, Oklahoma, Christina Adams was talking to a family friend who had temporarily been confined to a wheelchair after hip replacement surgery. It was a hot summer, and when the friend perspired, he got rashes because his skin stayed damp where it came in contact with the wheelchair. Christina listened to his complaint, decided to study the problem for her science fair project, then made three different models. She wanted to create something that would prevent pressure sores, the number-one health problem for people in wheelchairs. The sores can start in as few as three hours. Some people even die because the sores are so resistant to healing.

First, Christina made a wheelchair seat cover by layering absorbent and nonabsorbent fabrics, so that the layer of fabric next to the person would stay dry. That helped somewhat.

Then Christina decided to redesign the actual wheelchair seat. She worked with big sheets of plastic, heated them in the oven, and shaped them into a seat. After drilling holes in the plastic to let air through, she tested the wheelchair seat with a hygrometer, which measures humidity, and found that her seat with the holes was much cooler than the usual wheelchair seat. There was only one problem. Since her new wheelchair seat didn't fold, it wouldn't be easy to move from place to place.

The next year, Christina made a wheelchair seat out of adjustable criss-cross straps, like those on a backpack. The seat stays cool and dry because of the spaces between the straps. If a seated person feels pressure in any spot, the straps can easily be adjusted to relieve the pressure. It was a brand-new idea for a wheelchair seat and cost only about $50 to make, much less than existing seats.

"The biggest thing I learned from my experience," said Christina, "is that if you see a problem and you don't know how to solve the full problem, just start where you can, and as you work, new opportunities or new solutions start showing up. Just by starting, you learn more and more about it as you go and are better able to deal with it." Christina placed third in the engineering category at the 2001 Intel Science and Engineering Fair for the Adjustable Matrix Wheelchair Seat and also gained a patent for it and for the Moisture Dispersing Seat Cover for a Wheelchair. In 2001, she was inducted into the National Gallery for America's Young Inventors. ■

Inventors are usually optimists. When faced with failure or obstacles, they keep on plugging away because they believe they can make their inventions work.

When they begin a project, inventors usually identify a problem, imagine a solution, make a sketch of what they want to create, and think about the materials and the skills they need to start working.

Start with a Sketch

The first step in making a model is to sketch or draw your idea in your inventor's log or journal. You can do simple or complicated sketches. The important thing is that the sketch should illustrate your idea clearly and be easy to understand. If you were to look at it later and find it confusing, the sketch wouldn't be very helpful.

Many inventors label or number each part of a sketch or a drawing. Then, they make notes about the sketch as a whole and about the labeled or numbered parts in particular. They describe what each part does or how it interacts with other parts. Try to do that, and jot down any other thoughts about the sketches as well. You can also sketch different views of your invention—front view, back view, side view, and top view.

Make a List of Materials

Next, ask yourself, "What materials will I need to make my idea into a model?" You don't have to use new materials. You can find all sorts of supplies around the house, in junkyards, and at thrift stores or yard sales, or you can get them through relatives or neighbors. Models of many complicated inventions can be made with simple, inexpensive materials. You don't necessarily need to spend a lot of money. Many inventors use simple materials that are close at hand just to prove that an idea works, knowing that they can use better materials later for the finished product.

The Illuminated Nut Driver

Kristin Hrabar, of Aberdeen, New Jersey, used a battery-powered penlight, a straw, and a nut to make a model of her Illuminated Nut Driver. Kristin came up with the idea for this invention when she was nine. Her father, Frank Hrabar, had asked her to hold a flashlight so that he could see while tightening a nut underneath the clothes dryer. Her family later manufactured a more elaborate product based on her idea, using different materials and a sturdier construction (available at www.laserdriverstore.com), but her inexpensive working model, made of simple materials, proved that the idea worked and showed how. In 2002, Kristin participated in a television show called *Inventors' Showdown*, which aired on the Discovery Channel in June of that year. She also gained a patent for her invention. ∎

Kristin Hrabar with her Illuminated Nut Driver.

List the Tools You Will Need

Once you have a list of needed materials, think of what tools you will need to put it all together. Can you manage with some simple ones, such as a screwdriver, a wrench, pliers, or scissors? Or will you need an electric drill, a band saw, a welding tool, or a sewing machine? Will you need access to a computer? What will it take to engineer your idea? Make notes in your log or journal about all the tools you'll need. If you don't have access to these tools or the skills to use them, start thinking about how you can gain access to the tools and who can teach you how to use them.

Estimate Costs

With notes and sketches about your ideas and lists of needed materials, tools, and skills written in your inventor's log or journal, you're all set to begin working on your model. Right? Stop for a minute. What's it going to cost? Can you afford to make a model of the idea you have in mind? Add up the cost of everything you think you need. If the cost is beyond your budget, think about how you could cut costs. Find used or scrap materials, or see if someone could donate some of the materials. Or earn a little money to fund your project by washing cars, making deliveries, designing Web pages, or doing any other odd job. Or pick a more affordable idea. Cost is also measured in time. Estimate how long the project may take you. Try not to embark on something that you won't be able to afford or finish.

Inventory Your Skills and Acquire Others

Inventors use all sorts of skills in making a model. The ability to take good notes, measure and cut, paint, and take photos are all important skills. So are welding, sawing, gardening, sewing, and cooking. It can also help to have some knowledge of electricity, physics, chemistry, or computers. Many classes are offered not only at schools but also by local colleges, cities, clubs, and youth organizations and camps. If you don't have the necessary skills to make your invention, don't be discouraged. Many inventors learn skills as they invent.

The Rain Watchdog

Johnny Bodylski, of Tustin, California, was only seven years old when he created a device for automatically turning off the sprinklers when it rains. "It's basically a see-saw," said Johnny. He set up a wooden balance beam on a stand with a sliding set of weights (made of washers and a bolt) on one end and a cottage cheese container cup on the other end. He installed a micro-switch under the cup. Rainfall filling the cup would cause the cup to hit the micro-switch and turn off the timer. Later, as the water evaporated, the cup would rise and release the switch. That allowed the timer to turn back on.

Johnny asked his dad to teach him the skills needed to make his invention work. "What's neat about my dad is that he knows how to make things," said Johnny. "That makes it easier for me because I can go in and say, 'I need to do this, this, and this.' He'll say, 'Okay, this is how you do this. This is how you do that. Now take it and run.' Most of what I know about electronics and mechanics comes from him." Johnny did experiments to determine how much water was needed to depress the cup so that it would hit the switch. He observed how his device worked and made adjustments. He was chosen in 1996 as one of the original inductees into the National Gallery for America's Young Inventors. He called his device the Rain Watchdog. "I like the name," said Johnny, "because it hints at the sense of protection that a watchdog gives. It watches over your lawn so you don't have to." ■

Set Up a Workshop

Just as it's important to have a study desk where you do your homework, it's a good idea to have a workspace to make models and inventions. Some young inventors do their work at school. Others work in their rooms, at the kitchen table, in the basement, in the yard, or in the garage.

The Speed Grain Cart

Justin Riebeling, of Millstadt, Illinois, adapted a small wagon into a tool that would make it easier to do his daily chore of carrying buckets of feed weighing approximately 25 pounds each to the family's fifteen cows. His family's garage served as a workshop, and Justin had access to many tools and a place to measure, cut, and do other work. He started out by measuring 1-foot-high pieces of wood to make sides for the wagon that would hold the feed. His dad cut the wood for him and helped him attach these to the wagon. That could have been enough, but Justin wanted a sliding door on one side so that when it was raised, the feed would pour into the cow's trough. When his dad pointed out that the feed wouldn't slide out very easily, Justin got the idea of putting a 45-degree angle wooden slide inside the wagon. Then he decided to line the slide and the entire inside of the wagon with sheet metal, making it

Justin Riebeling with the Speed Grain Cart.

really smooth. He attached a bar to the door so that when he pushed down on the bar, the door went up and the grain easily slid out. At school, his classmates were impressed. "They thought I was going to win the science fair and that it was really neat," said Justin. "I'm not the smartest guy alive. I just get Bs and Cs. They're like, 'How did you come up with it?'" Justin was a 2002 national finalist in the Craftsman/NSTA Young Inventors Program and was a 2003 inductee into the National Gallery for America's Young Inventors. ■

Ask for Help and Be Safe

Sometimes you might have a great idea, but making a working model of your idea requires special equipment or tools that you don't know how to use, aren't able to use, or aren't allowed to use because they're dangerous. Other people can help. Ask an adult to instruct and observe you while you use the tools. Safety procedures are an important part of model making and inventing. Or, perhaps an adult will agree to do the task according to your specifications.

Many inventors ask others for help. Just be sure that you do the work that you're capable of (if you have the skills) and that you do the thinking. Although others may help you, the ideas should be yours.

The Easy Door Assist

"Every time I go to Grandma's house, I have to hold the door open for her wheelchair, so I thought about inventing something to hold the door open automatically," said Katelyn Eubank, of Indianola, Iowa. She got the idea to attach paint rollers onto the wheels of her grandma's chair. The rollers would stick out vertically from the sides of the chair and, without harming the door, keep the door open as her grandma's wheelchair passed through it. "I knew I wanted to invent something to help humans or animals," she said. Katelyn measured all of the materials, and her dad did the welding. "The first time we made it, the wheelchair wouldn't fit through the door, so we had to narrow it," said Katelyn. "Then, it pushed inward and hit the wheels. The next time we made it a little bit stronger. We worked together. I got frustrated because we had to redo it several times and I didn't think it would ever turn out, but it did. Don't let frustration make you stop trying." Katelyn won scholarships at the 2003 Invent Iowa and the 2004 Craftsman/NSTA Young Inventors Awards Program. ■

Inventor's Tip

"I wore safety goggles, a thick long-sleeved shirt, and protective leather gloves when using the drill, to protect myself from being hurt by flying metal."

—*Kevin Sellars, national winner, 2004 Invent America! Student Invention Contest for the Retractable Bicycle Fender*

Sometimes you don't have the skills or the ability to use a certain machine or piece of equipment or even the access to it, and neither does anyone in your family. If you need to use sophisticated equipment that is not easily available, you can ask your teacher, mentor, or parent to arrange access to equipment that may be owned by a local university or institution. Or you might pay to have a certain task performed, in order to realize your idea.

The Sweep Stopper

Matthew Christiansen was a seventh-grader who lived on a farm in the town of Scranton, Iowa, that has a population of only five hundred. He invented the Sweep Stopper. It is used inside large grain bins, some of which hold more than 5,000 pounds of grain and are the size of a classroom. The sweep is an armlike device surrounded by curved metal that goes around and around inside the bin. It pushes grain toward an exit tunnel when it is time to sell or use the grain. "The sweep is pressurized to help stay up against the grain," said Matthew, "but there's always a certain amount of grain left behind, so my father, my brother, Randy, or I go behind the sweep, sweeping the floor down." This system is fine for Matt and his family and for many other farmers —that is, until very little grain is left in the bin. Then the sweep has nothing to stop it—except maybe the farmers' legs. "It scares all of us when we get to the bottom of those bins," Matthew's dad explained. "If you're in the bin cleaning up, you can get tangled up in it really easily."

Matthew's invention is a simple piece of metal bent at a 90-degree angle that blocks the path of the wheel at the end of the sweep. The idea was that when the sweep started to move too fast, it would hit the Sweep Stopper and stop. Yet, Matthew did not have the ability to bend a piece of metal. He paid a person who was experienced in working with metal to do the job. He had the idea. Someone else had the machinery and skill to make it a reality. Matthew installed Sweep Stoppers in all six bins on the family farm. Other farmers in town are interested in having them as well. Matthew won a scholarship for his invention at the 2003 Invent Iowa competition. ∎

Individual students often get help from parents, teachers, mentors, and other experts, but if you work as a team with a coach, this can sometimes give you access to expert advice.

The Stopping Cart

Four seventh-graders from Brandon Middle School in Brandon, Mississippi, with the help of their coach, teacher Joe Ann Clark, decided to address the problem of runaway shopping carts in store parking lots. The students, Patricia Rincon, Lauren Rushing, Joel Anderson, and Patrick Hall, talked to managers of several stores, including Home Depot and Wal-Mart, and asked whether they had any problems with shopping carts and how much it cost them to pay for damage done to cars due to wayward carts. "One official told us that they pay an average of $5,000 per store yearly nationwide in claims related to shopping cart damage to cars in their parking lots," said team member Lauren Rushing.

The Stopping Cart team began to design a brake for shopping carts, and along the way they sought advice from mechanical engineers at Mississippi State University. "A NASA scientist met with them and played the devil's advocate," said Joe Ann Clark. "They had their design, but he made them work through the details, to make sure they knew what they were doing." The resulting brake consisted of a metal bar that ran parallel to the cart's push bar. When you push the bar down, it disengages the brakes. Let it go, and it stops the cart. The students tested the brakes with heavy and light loads and on inclines. It worked every time. One judge, Greg Hale, vice president of ride and show engineering at Walt Disney World, called their design "elegant engineering" and said the invention was "ready to go." The team garnered first place at the 2002 Christopher Columbus Awards. ■

Make a Scale Model

Sometimes you might have an idea for something grand, such as a way to prevent helicopter crashes. You might consider making a scale model to test your idea. A scale model is an object, usually built to scale (reduced or increased according to a fixed proportion), that represents in detail another, usually larger object. Scale models of airplanes are used to test many new ideas for improving flight. Engineers use scale models of bridges or buildings to test ideas. Making and using a scale model is one of your options.

Active Spin Control: The Next Step after Anti-Lock Brakes

KIDS INVENTING!

"I have always been interested in cars, especially electric ones," wrote Hans Christiansen Lee, of Carmel, California, in a report about his invention that would keep cars from skidding out of control. At the time, he was a senior in high school. "In the fifth grade I started to build an electric car. I worked on the car for about five years and got the frame, suspension, and drive train mostly built. My idea was not to finish the car, but to learn as much as I could about physics and building cars." While he was doing that, he learned how to use power tools such as drills and a band saw. His dad, an engineer, mentored him on many of his projects, and Hans learned about circuitry and computer programming, as well as engineering. He learned how to write technical reports from his mother.

During high school, he worked for a company that designed electronic controllers and motors, and he thought of a way to keep cars from skidding. He wanted to prove his idea, but he couldn't work on an actual car because of cost and safety issues. He decided to use a smaller vehicle—a go-cart.

After installing independently controlled motors on the rear wheels of the go-cart, he used his welding skills to build mounting brackets an electronic control circuit, an integrated circuit. Hans then programmed the computer so that when the go-cart was out of control—spinning or skidding—it sent a message to the rear motors to put the vehicle back under control. With his system, when the go-cart started to skid, Hans didn't have to apply the brakes. The computer did it for him.

"Driving the go-cart was a blast," Hans said. "It wasn't dangerous. The go-cart was very stable." Hans's system, Active Spin Control: The Next Step after Anti-Lock Brakes, activated quickly—within 2 inches when the vehicle was going 60 miles per hour, much faster than other anti-skid control systems that rely on the engine to initiate the stop. "Every day people die in single-car accidents, and many are probably caused by loss of control," said Hans. "Surely, decreasing the number of these accidents would save lives and money."

Hans was a national finalist in the 2000 Siemens Westinghouse Competition in Math, Science & Technology, and he won a $20,000 college scholarship at the Intel Science Talent Search. In 2001, he was inducted into the National Gallery for America's Young Inventors. He was featured as one of the "Twenty Teens Who Will Change the World" by *Teen People* magazine in 2002. ■

Inventor's Tip

"Don't give up if something doesn't work out or go just the way it's planned. Keep trying new things if you hit a speed bump. Never give up. My invention was a class project. Set aside the grade, I just wanted to make it work, so I was going to keep working until it did."

—Lindsey Clement, 2001 inductee into the National Gallery for America's Young Inventors for the Gumball Machine

Activities

1. Get Ready to Build Your Invention

   Use the steps in the chapter to start your project:

   • Draw a sketch of your invention idea.

   • Determine, then gather the materials and the tools you'll need.

   • Set up a workshop. Set aside an area, even a small one, to store your materials and assemble your invention.

2. Make a Device

   Many skills are easy once you learn them. Learn a new skill or try using your current skills to combine two of the items listed on the next page. For example, make a lighted pet collar or a hammer with an attached magnet to hold nails. You'll improve your skills in the process and be better prepared to make your invention. If you don't yet have an idea for an invention, perhaps you can create one from these different items.

wheels	springs	handle	broom
magnets	whistle	shovel	rope
lights	door	rake	CD
Velcro	ball	dust pan	shirt

3. Make a Scale Model

   Making a scale model (an object that represents in detail another, usually larger object) can help you understand more clearly how something works. Try using simple materials to make a scale model of a hovercraft or a paper car.

   HOVERCRAFT

   Make a simple hovercraft out of just a few items.

   Materials

   glue

   plastic top used on many water bottles or energy drinks
   (the type with a part that pulls up to allow for drinking and
   pushes down to keep the liquid from spilling)

   CD

   balloon

   Instructions

   1. Glue the plastic top over the hole in the CD.
   2. Push down the movable part of the plastic top so that it won't admit air.
   3. Blow up the balloon and place it over the closed top.
   4. Pull open the top to allow the air to escape from the balloon.
   5. Let go. Watch the CD/hovercraft propel across the floor.

   Think of the bigger picture. How could you apply the properties of this simple hovercraft to other devices or to your invention?

   PAPER CAR

   Construct a car that will roll. Make it out of paper, glue, wooden skewers, and a few other materials. The maximum dimensions for your paper car are 2½ inches wide, 6 inches long, and 3 inches high.

   Materials

   graph paper

   four sheets of 20 lb. 8½ × 11-inch paper

   pen or pencil

   scissors

glue (glue stick or tape)

ruler

two index cards

compass

one plastic straw

two wooden skewers (or two large paper clips that have been uncurled)

Instructions

A. Design the Car

   1. Design the car that you want to build. (If you find a photo of a car you would like to build, use graph paper and chart the scale of the photo, then reduce or enlarge the scale to make your car.) Remember, your construction doesn't have to be perfect. It should just look like a car and be able to roll.

   2. Draw a sketch of the car you would like to build. Your drawing should be a profile, showing the side of the car (the view you would see if you were watching it pass by). Be sure your drawing doesn't exceed the maximum dimensions stated earlier.

B. Make the Body

   1. Make the sides of the car. Cut out six "car-sides," or profiles, of the car. Each side should be exactly the same size and shape. Apply glue to one of the sides and lay one of the other sides on top of it. Then, apply glue to that side and lay a third side on top, creating a paper-and-glue sandwich that is three layers thick. Let dry. (Tip: put a heavy book or other object on top of the sides as they dry so they will be flat. Protect the book or object by putting wax paper on either side of the paper-and-glue creation.) As the glue dries, it will harden; this is known as the lamination process. The sides will be sturdier than ones made only of paper. You've just made one side of your car. Repeat the process for the other three car-sides.

   2. Make the bottom of the car. Measure and cut two pieces of paper that will be as wide as the bottom of the car you are making. Measure and cut a third piece of paper that is half an inch wider and longer than the other two pieces. Glue the first two pieces together for rigidity as you did with the sides. Since the third piece is half an inch larger than the other two, glue it to the other pieces last, leaving a quarter-inch edge that is not glued and is pliable. Let dry. Fold the quarter-inch margin up. Apply glue and press the paper margin to the bottom of your car-sides. Let dry. You now have a rigid, three-dimensional piece.

   3. Make the top of the car. As you did with the bottom, measure the paper before you cut it so as to make the top half an inch wider than the width of the car and to have a quarter-inch margin on all edges. You will have to

cut the paper and shape it to form the top. To make folds for the fenders, the hood, or the trunk, you can cut out diamond or triangular pieces at the folds so that the paper is easier to shape. Once you have the form, fold a quarter-inch margin on all the edges. Glue that strip and attach the top to the sides and bottom of the car.

C. Make and Attach the Wheels

1. While you can create wheels to scale, they may be too small to function well on a small paper car. You might try making them a bit bigger than scale. Use the index cards as the material for the wheels. The wheels should be about the size of a quarter or a lid for a baby food jar. Use one of those objects to trace the shape of the wheels on the index cards. Cut out eight wheels. As you did with the sides, glue two of the circles together to make one wheel. (The glue in between the index cards makes for a stronger, sturdier wheel.) Let dry. Use a compass point, a pen, or a pencil to punch a small hole in the middle of the wheel. Repeat the process for the other three wheels.

2. Cut two pieces from the straw that you will glue to the bottom of the car at the front and the back to hold the axles for the wheels in place. Cut pieces that are almost as wide as the bottom of the car (95 percent of the width).

3. Glue the straw pieces to the bottom of the car at the front and the back.

4. Insert one wooden skewer (the axle) into one of the straw pieces.

5. Attach a wheel to one end of the skewer (axle). Secure with glue. Let dry. Attach the second wheel. Secure with glue. Let dry. Repeat on the other side.

Your car is now ready for decorating. You can cut out spaces for windows or paint it. You can also add bumpers, an exhaust pipe, a grille, or an antenna.

Once your car is decorated to your liking, it's ready for a test drive. Place the car on a slanted surface. Let it roll. Get your friends to make one, too, and have a race.

How could you improve your scale model? Did you learn any tricks in making it that you could apply to your invention model?

Here are some alternate ideas for your paper car:

- Make the car out of cardstock. Use tape instead of glue to attach the pieces.
- Experiment by making the top of the car out of papier mache or other materials.

4

Naming Your Invention

Naming your invention is often a really fun part of the invention process. You might name the invention after yourself. You could name it by what it does, looks like, or sounds like. Maybe you'll name it for its ingredients or the materials it's made of. Or you might just choose a catchy name. Frank Epperson first called his creation the Ep-sicle, a combination of his name and the word *icicle*. You know it as the Popsicle. He invented it in 1905, when he was eleven. On a cold night, he left his drink outside on the porch with the stir stick in it. He wanted to see how it would taste frozen. He liked the results, but it wasn't until 1923 that he began selling the treat. His children later changed the name to combine their name for him, Pop, with *icicle*.

Name Your Invention after Yourself

Kellogg's Corn Flakes was named for Will Keith Kellogg, the man who created the flaky breakfast cereal. Totino's Pizza is named for Rose Totino, the woman who invented a way to freeze pizza. Pasteurized milk is named for Louis Pasteur, who created a way to destroy microorganisms in milk. Lots of inventions, even kids' inventions, include the name of the inventor.

Charlie's Automatic Dog Washer

Charlie Matykiewicz, of Windermere, Florida, was thirteen when he invented an automatic dog washer. It was a boxlike frame made out of PVC pipe. A collar on one of the top pipes kept his dog, Candy, in place. A hose attached to a bottom pipe provided the water. When Charlie turned on the hose, water sprayed out in jets through nozzles that he had fitted into holes he'd drilled in the pipes. Candy got cleaner without the trouble and the mess. Charlie called his invention Charlie's Automatic Dog Washer. ■

Name Your Invention for What It Does

Charlie's Automatic Dog Washer not only tells you who invented it, it also tells you what it does. Many inventions are named for what we do with them or what they do. A fly swatter is a piece of plastic on a stick that's used to swat flies. The computer adds up information: in other words, it computes. What about the paper clip? Sometimes the simple names are the easiest to remember. One young inventor picked a very simple descriptive name for his invention.

The Pedal Powered Lawn Mower

Mitchell Weiss, a seventh-grader from Bloomfield, Connecticut, found out that he was a winner in the 2001 Craftsman/NSTA Young Inventors Awards Program (sponsored by Sears) when he heard the name of his invention announced at a school assembly. As he sat in the audience, a guest speaker from the nearby Sears store spoke. "He asked, 'How many people have heard of a hammer?' and everyone raised their hands,'" remembered Mitchell. "And then he asked 'How many people have heard of a screwdriver?' And again everyone raised his or her hand, and then he asked, 'Now, how many of you have heard of a Pedal Powered Lawn Mower?' Right then, I was completely shocked, and I felt like all the blood had run from my face," Mitchell said. That was the name of his invention. He had made it by replacing the front wheel of a bicycle with a push mower. It makes cutting the grass easy because all you have to do is ride a bike. ■

Mitchell Weiss's Pedal Powered Lawn Mower.

Use Word Tricks in Naming Your Invention

Mitchell used a word trick in the name of his invention: two of the words—Pedal and Powered—begin with the same sounds. That trick or technique is called alliteration—for example, Happy Holidays, best bet, or Simple Simon. It's a neat word trick and can lead to a nifty name.

Inventor's Tip

"A name needs to describe the invention, be catchy, be remembered easily, and be fun to say."

—Austin Meggitt, 1999 inductee into the National Gallery for America's Young Inventors for the Glove and Battie Caddie

The Bendable Broom

Peter Hosinski, a fourth-grader at Davenport School in Stamford, Connecticut, used alliteration when he named his invention, the Bendable Broom, a tool that lets you sweep in those hard-to-reach spots. He was a finalist in the 2001 Craftsman/NSTA Young Inventors Awards Program. ■

Rhyming is another word trick. That's the technique of using words that sound like one another, such as *true*, *blue*, and *you*.

The Fair Share Timer

When Betsy Armitage was in second grade at Holmes Elementary School in San Diego, California, she created the Fair Share Timer, a giant egg timer made of two liter-size soda bottles with a wooden platform on either end. To make her invention, Betsy experimented until the sand took exactly five minutes to pass from one bottle to the other. She got the idea for the timer because she and her sisters were always arguing about how long either of them had been on the trampoline in their yard. When she named her invention, Betsy used rhyming words: *fair* and *share*. The rhyme sounds good and adds to the meaning of the name. She was a national finalist in the 2003 Craftsman/NSTA Young Inventors Awards Program. ■

Making up your own words is another naming trick. Lots of combinations of letters don't mean anything, but they sound kind of cool when used to make a word, like *-itz* or *-oogle*. Flip-Itz, for example, is the name of a toy that flips. You can combine two words in a new way or even create totally new words to name your invention.

E-colocator Gloves

Seventh-graders at John Burroughs School in St. Louis, Missouri, won first place in the 2004 ExploraVision program for envisioning a future invention. Their idea is for gloves that would be worn by meat handlers and restaurant workers. The gloves would quickly change color when they came in contact with meat infected with *E. coli* bacteria. They named the gloves E-colocator Gloves. The name combines the words *E. coli* and *locator*, a name that is easy to remember and comments about the detection capability of the gloves. Pretty clever! ■

Carthritis

Charles Johnson, of Hamilton, Texas, who entered and won invention contests almost every year from kindergarten through high school, used word tricks in naming a lever device. He created it so that his grandmother, who suffered from arthritis, could easily turn on her car ignition. He called it Carthritis, a combination of *car* and *arthritis*. The invention worked, too. His grandmother used it for years, and Charles won the Inventor of the Year award at a local Invention Convention and was national champion of the Invent America! Student Invention Contest in 1996. ■

Inventor's Tip

"A name should be for what your invention is, what it is used for, and sometimes the inventor's name. A girl in my class invented Julie's Wrap-O-Matic to help you wrap with plastic wrap. It describes what it does and who it belongs to. That's a good name."

—*Luke Bader, Meritorious Award winner, Invent Iowa 2003 State Invention Convention for the Walk Along*

Name Your Invention for Its Sound

If your invention makes a sound, like a click, a snap, a whoosh, or a pop, you can use a word that describes this in the name of your invention. Charles Johnson named another of his inventions for its sound. The Baby Buzzer was a pressure sensor placed at the bottom and the top of a stairway, which would buzz if a baby tried to crawl up or down the stairs.

Dalton Adams, a fourth-grader at Rheems Elementary School in Rheems, Pennsylvania, called his invention Snap-a-Flag because the American flag is on a shade that snaps when it rolls up or down, to store it or display it. He was a regional winner in the 2003 Craftsman/NSTA Young Inventors Awards Program.

Name Your Invention for Its Feel

If your invention has a certain feel, refer to that in its name. Maybe it's soft and cuddly, has sharp edges or a rough surface, or is spiky or spongy. Seventh-graders Brittney

Kaonohi and Kimmy Stoll, of McLoud, Oklahoma, picked the name Ruff-n-Tuffies for the rubber gloves they designed that have sponges and scrubbers built into the fingers and palms. They were second-place winners in the 2003 Invent America! Student Invention Contest.

Give Your Invention a Catchy Name

Some inventions have catchy names that describe the invention but add a twist. Sometimes it takes a while to remember the name, but once you do, the name is hard to forget. Slinky is the name of a toy, a spring that "walks." Many kids love to watch it walk down stairs. Yet during World War II, U.S. Naval engineer Richard James discovered quite accidentally that a spring could be a toy when he was experimenting with springs and one fell to the ground and started moving. Later, when he showed the lively spring to his wife, Betty, she looked in the dictionary and found the word *slink*, which means stealthy, sneaky, and sinuous. The name stuck, and Slinky debuted as a toy in 1946 and is still popular.

Kids have come up with other catchy names.

Inventor's Tip

"My job of feeding the cows was a slow process. For my model I used a wagon that can also be called a cart. I thought, 'This is a lot faster.' So I called it the Speed Grain Cart."

—*Justin Riebeling, 2003 inductee into the National Gallery for America's Young Inventors for the Speed Grain Cart*

Cactus Makes Perfect

Eight-year-old Sierra Jones, of San Diego, California, invented a cone-shaped plastic tool to wrap around cactus during planting. She dubbed it Cactus Makes Perfect. Sierra, who made her invention in 2003 for her third-grade class at Holmes Elementary School, said she thought of the name "because it reminds you that when you have to plant cactus, you have to practice and practice to do it without hurting yourself." ■

One type of catchy name is an acronym, such as VIP (very important person), DJ (disc jockey), or SCUBA (self-contained underwater breathing apparatus). The name is made up of the first letter of each word of a longer name.

HEADS UP

Harris Sokoloff was a freshman at Northern Valley Regional High School in Demarest, New Jersey, when he got an assignment to create a battery-powered invention for his electronics technology class. That same day, he rode his bike home while listening to music on his headphones. He was thinking hard and the music drowned out all background noise, so he didn't hear the car honking—the one that almost hit him.

"Luckily, I didn't get hurt, so I was able to think it would have been nice if I'd been able to hear the car," said Harris. "That's where the idea came from."

Harris spent several months creating a sound-detecting device, which attaches to a portable CD player. When a sound—such as a car horn—is detected, the device sends a signal to a relay that trips a voice recorder. "Before using the device," said Harris, "the wearer records his or her own personalized message via the microphone built into the device. When the device detects the loud noise, it plays that message in the headphones, like 'Danger!' or 'Watch out!'

"My teacher, Mr. Rabelo, set me on the right track once I had the idea," continued Harris. "He told me what I needed to do and roughly how to make it happen. Without his help, I wouldn't have made it."

To find out whether his device might help others, Harris e-mailed police departments around the country. Members of the Los Angeles Police Department contacted him and said that although they didn't have any hard data, they knew of many accidents that had resulted from people being unable to hear because of their headphones. For his efforts, Harris was inducted into the National Gallery for America's Young Inventors in 2002.

Harris wanted to name his device after what it does: warning people. Think about it. What do you say to people when you want them to pay attention? After he and his teacher made a list of fifty names, they both chose HEADS UP. It's catchy, but it's also an acronym for the descriptive name: Headphone Emergency Alert Defense System. Clever, isn't it? ∎

Harris Sokoloff with the display for his HEADS UP warning device.

Inventor's Tip

"An important thing in naming is to make it logical. If you figure out a name that is descriptive and catchy at the same time, you have a balance."

—*Charles Johnson, national champion, 1996 Invent America! Student Invention Contest for the Train Detecting Device.*

Activities

1. Name an Invention by Using Your Name

   How can you make your name fit with the name of an invention? Try using word tricks and descriptive words to combine your name with other words and come up with a great new name. Can you rhyme your first or last name with a word that is part of the product name? Or can you use alliteration to combine your name with a product name? For example, Betsy's Backpack.

2. Rename Some Well-Known Inventions

   Think of other names for some familiar items: snowboard, skateboard, computer mouse, hair brush, bike pump, washing machine, microwave oven, or refrigerator.

3. Have Fun with a Rhyming Dictionary

   Select an assortment of different products in your room, the kitchen, or the garage. Then, use your rhyming dictionary to find words that rhyme with the product names. Do any of the rhymed names add up to a better name for the product?

4. Think of an Acronym

   Write a descriptive name for an invention or your own invention and then see if you can create a word out of each of the first letters of the descriptive name. For example, ACTION could be the name of nutritious cookie shaped like an action hero. The acronym could stand for Action Character That Increases Our Nutrition.

5

Participating in Competitions, Programs, and Camps

Opportunities abound for young inventors. Schools, clubs, organizations, companies, cities, states, and countries all encourage invention. Some ask for inventions that benefit the environment or the community. Others ask for inventions that are toys or tools. Yet others are open-ended and ask only, "What can you invent?" In 1919, thirteen-year-old Philo Farnsworth won a national contest sponsored by Hugo Gernsback's *Science and Invention* magazine for coming up with a magnetized ignition and key. He entered because he had decided before he was twelve that he would rather be an inventor than a farmer. Yet it was while he was working in the sugar beet fields on his family's farm that he got the idea for inventing the device we know as television. He started working on his idea in high school and later gained 160 of the more than a thousand patents that led to the perfection of this entertainment medium.

While many students who enter invention fairs also enter science fairs, it's important to understand the difference between the two types of fairs. Science fairs prompt students to conduct experiments, create systems or machines, or do research on certain topics. Their results may or may not result in inventions. Winning students are rewarded for their science skills, talent, and accomplishments. Invention fairs require that all entries be inventions. Entrants often use math and science skills as they work, but one of the steps is to determine that their idea is an invention.

Most students start by creating inventions as class assignments. Then, they present their inventions at

Inventor's Tip

"The funny thing is that at my local Invention Convention, I only got an honorable mention and I was kind of discouraged. That's when I saw a national contest in a magazine. I entered and won first place."

—Johnny Bodylski, 1996 inductee into the National Gallery for America's Young Inventors for the Rain Watchdog

school fairs. Sometimes students who win and some who don't win at a school fair enter their inventions in city, county, statewide, national, or international contests. Some students enter several inventions in various competitions. An invention that doesn't appeal to one set of judges may be the choice of another set. Many students who have gotten an honorable mention in one contest go on to garner first or second place in another. It happens all the time. Take advantage of the opportunity to enter lots of competitions.

Invention programs vary. Some competitions are open only to individuals, others only to teams. While most contests are entered through schools, others are geared toward individual students, with or without teacher advisers. Some programs are for students in grades K through 12, and others only for kids in lower grades or upper grades. Countries around the world sponsor contests for students, and some of these accept applicants internationally. You could enter several ideas, each to a different program.

What You Can Gain by Entering an Invention Contest

Many competitions offer cash prizes, gifts, savings bonds, or scholarships to the winners. Some young inventors gain patents and trademarks and then license or sell their inventions. Some use their inventions as stepping-stones to gain internships, scholarships, or consideration by college admission boards. Most young inventors benefit personally by creating an invention and presenting it to judges. The experience boosts their confidence and self-esteem.

Inventor's Tip

"If there were no competitions or monetary rewards, I'd do it all over again. You learn so much when you are committed to a project. It's a great learning experience."

—Kavita Shukla, 2001 inductee into the National Gallery for America's Young Inventors for Fenugreek-Treated Paper

Preparing for Competition

Read the Guidelines

Since each competition is unique, carefully read the guidelines before you start so that you understand the goal and what you're being asked to provide. Does the program or the competition call for just an idea and an explanation, or does it also ask for a working model? Does it call for background research? Does it ask entrants to work with the community? Does it ask for the creation of a Web site? Think about the skills you have and the ones you need to compete in different programs. For example, here are the guidelines for the Craftsman/NSTA Young Inventors Awards Program:

> Students in grades two through eight must work independently with guidance from adults to invent and build a tool or modify an existing one, document

their progress in an inventor's log, provide a diagram of the tool, a photo of the student using the tool and a completed entry form. For example, a tool to open a door, to make it easier to put air in a soccer ball, to ride a scooter in the snow.

The guidelines for the Inventive Kids Around the World Contest, sponsored by Canada's Inventive Women, are quite different.

Children ages 7 through 12 from any country are eligible. They are asked to send an idea and a drawing of their invention or a photograph if they have actually built it. Inventions can be submitted in the following categories: inventions to improve safety, to help our environment, to improve everyday living, to help us stay healthy, or inventions that are weird and useful!

As with the Inventive Kids Around the World Contest, many competitions or programs have categories—computer science, the environment, health, safety, and so on. Decide which is the best category for your invention, or create an invention for a specific category. Either way, make sure that you don't submit a great project to the wrong category or to the wrong contest.

Make a List of Submission Requirements

Competitions and programs all have different submission requirements. Some ask students to submit an idea with an explanation. Others—such as many state or school fairs—ask for models, logs, and reports. With some online programs, you'll have to create a Web site instead of a display. Make sure that you know what you must submit. Why eliminate yourself by omitting one of the requirements? Include everything on the list.

Compare the requirements of the following two programs.

The Invent Iowa State Invention Convention asks for

- A display board that includes the name of the invention and the inventor
- A statement of the idea identified and the role of the invention in addressing it
- A diagram of the invention that provides evidence it will work and documentation that a similar invention does not exist
- A model or a prototype of the invention that provides evidence that it will work
- An inventor's log

Student Ideas for a Better America, a monthly contest open to students in grades K through 8 and 9 through 12, asks students to submit only an idea, not a model, for a new product or an improvement for an existing product. There are no set guidelines for submission. Ideas may be submitted on video- or audiotapes, in pictures, on slides, or on overheads.

You could enter both competitions, but you would have to assemble and submit different materials for each one.

INVENT IOWA Evaluation Rubric

LEVELS OF MASTERY

CRITERIA FOR INVENTION		Expert INVENTOR 5	Skillful INVENTOR 4	Amateur INVENTOR 3	Beginner INVENTOR 2	POINTS
Novelty	A. Does the invention involve a *novel idea*?	A significant level of difference between this invention and prior products **5**	A substantial level of difference between this invention and prior products **4**	Some simple differences between this invention and prior products **3**	Very similar to prior Products **2**	Novelty A ___ +
	B. Is the invention a *fresh or unexpected* idea?	Unique and exciting product idea **5**	Very interesting product idea **4**	Attractive but predictable idea **3**	Traditional product idea **2**	B ▢ =
Usefulness	C. Is the invention *workable*?	Clear and convincing evidence that this invention will work effectively **5**	Sufficient evidence that this invention will work effectively **4**	Minimal evidence that this invention will work effectively **3**	Little evidence that this invention will work effectively **2**	Useful C ___ +
	D. Is the invention *appropriate* for the stated need or idea?	A clear and convincing connection between the problem or idea and the invention **5**	Sufficient evidence of a connection between the problem or ideas and the invention **4**	Minimal evidence of a connection between the problem or idea and the invention **3**	Little evidence of a connection between the problem or idea and the invention **2**	D ▢ =
Appeal	E. Does the invention have strong *interest and appeal* to intended audience?	Professional in appearance and well-suited to the intended audiences **5**	Attractive and useful for the intended audiences **4**	Useful to some people in the intended audience **3**	Idea might have potential interest and appeal **2**	Appeal E ___ +
	F. Is the invention *well-crafted and complete*?	Clear and convincing evidence that materials and construction are the best for the invention **5**	Sufficient evidence that materials and construction can be used for the invention **4**	Minimal evidence that materials and construction can be used for the invention **3**	Little evidence that materials and construction can be used for the invention **2**	F ▢ =
	Invention Point Subtotals	_____	_____	_____	_____	_____

Evaluation rubric for the Invent Iowa competition.

CRITERIA FOR ENTRY	*Expert* INVENTOR 5	*Skillful* INVENTOR 4	*Amateur* INVENTOR 3	*Beginner* INVENTOR 2	POINTS
G. Is the invention entry *diagram* presented professionally?	**Elaborate** and **attractive** diagram with all parts clearly labeled and explained — 5	An **attractive** diagram with all parts labeled — 4	Diagram with **most** parts labeled — 3	A **simple** drawing of the invention — 2	**Invention Presentation** G ____ +
H. (1) Is the invention entry *model* a clear idea representation?	A **highly-detailed** and **comprehensive** representation of the invention — 5	A **comprehensive** representation of the invention — 4	An **adequate** representation of the invention — 3	A **simplified** representation of the invention — 2	H (1) ____ +
OR					*OR*
H. (2) Is the invention entry *prototype* an exact replica?	A **highly-detailed** and **comprehensive** working replica of the invention — 5	A **comprehensive** working replica of the invention — 4	An **adequate** working replica of the invention — 3	A **simplified** working replica of the invention — 2	H (2) ____ +
I. Is the Inventor's *Log* thorough and complete?	A **well-developed** description of the invention process — 5	A **description** containing the **highlights** of the invention process — 4	Brief **statement** of the invention idea and solution — 3	A **partial description** of the invention — 2	I ____ +
J. Is the Inventor's *oral presentation* thorough and complete?	Communicates a **high level of knowledge** and **understanding of the process** leading to this invention — 5	Communicates **some knowledge** and **understanding of the process** leading to this invention — 4	**Describes** the invention **idea and the solution** — 3	**Briefly describes** the invention — 2	J ____ =
Entry Point Subtotals					[ ]

YIF JUDGING FORM

Please note: Ratings are only meaningful if the highest scores are reserved for exceptional work.

This form is not shared with students.

Directions: Check scoring key at the top of the table.
Circle a score for each item.

Entry form items:

	Does not meet basic requirements		Meets all requirements given		Exceeds requirements
1. Described the problem, situation or idea that led to the invention and told why other people would need or use the invention to make life easier or better. (8 pts.)	1	3	4	6	8
2. Described your invention and how it works (3 points). Included a photo of the invention. (2 points)	1	2	3	4	5
3. Provided a complete drawing of the invention including labels for every part and the dimensions. (5 points, computer drawings OK)	1	2	3	4	5
4. Listed all materials used to create the invention. (2 points)	0		1		2
5. Told about research done to find similar inventions. Listed at least 3 sources checked and told what was learned. Wrote down the names of any similar inventions found. (Total of 10 points, YIF Gazette is required and worth 3 points)	2	4	6	8	10
6. Told why the invention is a different or better way to do something. (10 points) Variations on past inventions are OK as long as this can be demonstrated.	2	4	6	8	10
7. Explained the step-by-step process used to design and build the invention, including any problems experienced. (8 points)	1	3	4	6	8
8. Described how the invention was tested to demonstrate it works effectively. Recorded the number of times it was tested and the name of a person who observed the testing. (8 points)	1	3	4	6	8
9. OPTIONAL QUESTION (0 points) Use this space for notes.					
10. OVERALL IMPRESSIONS: (10 points) The invention shows creativity in **one or more** of the following ways: A) original thinking, B) use of materials, C) the function of the invention, **and/or** D) unique qualities related to resourcefulness/playfulness or the invention's "personality."	2	4	6	8	10

Team # _____

Total Score _____
Rank # in team's box _____

Place forms in rank order in the team box with #1, the highest scored entry, placed on top.

Recommendation:

❏ Yes, exhibit at the Fair
❏ No, not recommended for exhibit
❏ Maybe exhibit at the Fair

1/2005

Judging form for the Young Inventors Program and Fair in the Twin Cities area of Minnesota.

Review the Judging Criteria

Various competitions ask young inventors to focus on different aspects or tools of invention. Compare the judging criteria of two team programs.

ExploraVision, a competition sponsored by Toshiba and the National Science Teachers Association and open to students in grades K through 12, asks students to study a present technology and envision its future. More points are given for information about future technology and designing Web pages than for information about present technology and history. Here's the breakdown of how the points are distributed: Present Technology (15 points), History (10 points), Future Technology (20 points), Breakthroughs (15 points), Consequences (15 points), Bibliography (5 points), and Web Page Graphics (20 points).

eCYBERMISSION, an online competition sponsored by the U.S. Army, asks students to use technology to solve a community problem and gives more points for using science, math, and technology than for creativity. The breakdown: Application of Science, Math, and Technology (40 percent); Innovation, Originality, and Creativity (20 percent); Benefit to the Community (20 percent); and Team Collaboration and Communication (20 percent).

Choose the competition where the judging criteria are the best match with your interests and skills.

Be Sure You Know the Deadline

What is the deadline for the entry? That's a very important date to know. Be sure to give yourself enough time to finish the project. If you don't send in your entry on time, it won't be accepted.

Planning a Display

Many contests ask for your project to be displayed. Most students use a piece of cardboard folded into three sections, which is available in office supply stores. On it, students paste photos, charts, or graphs that describe the invention. This display board will usually include the

name of the invention, a description of the problem, proof of why the idea is an invention, the experiments or the steps taken to make the model (if there is one), and information about the inventor. Typing the information in a 12-point black font makes for easy reading. Also, if the competition allows, make the headings or the titles of different sections of the display in several colors and in a larger font, 14 or 16 points or more.

Once you have everything that you want to put on the display board, lay it out but don't glue it down. Experiment with the arrangement, making sure not to leave any big white spaces. Ask your parents or friends for their opinions. When the arrangement looks impressive and well designed, carefully glue everything down.

Place your model, log, or report on a table in front of the display board. Just remember that you are not allowed to include anything potentially disruptive or dangerous in your display, such as animals, dangerous chemicals or other liquids, flames, bacteria or fungi, or sharp objects. If your invention involves these items, you can take photos and use them in your display.

Tips on Making a Display Board

- Design and print simple, clear titles.
- Make sure your written comments are easy to read for people who stop by your display.
- Have good, clear photos of the invention and of your progress or charts of your test results.
- Practice arranging the materials for the best visual presentation.

Prepare an Oral Presentation

You've written about your invention and included a model in your display, but can you also talk about it? Can you summarize the purpose of the invention in a few sentences? Can you tell the judges about your invention and why it's important? Can you give an example of how it would be useful to others? Or explain why it's new? These are the kinds of questions you'll need to answer while you stand in front of your display.

Let's admit it, you might get nervous. Presenting your invention can be a scary experience. Practice your answers before the competition, either with family or friends or in front of a mirror. Point to your display during your talk. If you point or hold a visual aid, this can often keep you from being nervous. You may be able to answer lots of questions about your project, but what if you can't answer every question? What should you do? Relax. Be honest, and tell whoever is asking that you don't know the answer, but you'll try to find out.

Inventor's Tip

"Always start your presentations with a WOW statement, a statement or question that gets everyone's attention. In my project I asked, "Did you know that millions of mosquitoes hatch every day and that they transmit some of the world's most deadly diseases?"

—*Peter Borden, 2003 national finalist, Discovery Channel Young Scientist Challenge for the Effect of Neem Oil on Mosquitoes*

Camps

Students enter invention contests and programs during the standard school year, but during the summer, many students take advantage of their free time to attend an invention, a math, or a science camp.

Camp Invention, a week-long summer day camp offered in more than forty-five states for children in the second through sixth grades, is a joint program of Invent Now and the National Inventors Hall of Fame. Kids Invent Toys! hosts one-week summer camps for elementary and middle school children in many states. A number of other camps sponsored by companies and organizations encourage kids to develop skills and knowledge of math, science, and technology to help them become better inventors.

Inventor's Tip

"Losing is not such a bad thing. Try to learn more about the winner's invention and think about what improvements you need to make to win the next time."

—*Christopher Cho, 1996 inductee into the National Gallery for America's Young Inventors for the Automatic Page-Replacing Contrivance*

Activities

1. Discover the Competitions

   Look in the appendix for the list of different invention competitions or programs. Check out the Web sites of the various programs. Which ones are you eligible to enter? Which winning inventions are really cool? Start thinking about what you could create for different programs.

2. Get Ready for Your Oral Presentation at the Invention Fair

   Do a five-minute presentation. In two minutes, introduce yourself and describe your invention. Explain how you made your model and proved your idea in another two minutes. Use one minute to explain why your idea is an invention.

6

Inventing as a Team

Teamwork works for everyone because you can share ideas as well as the work. In today's world, most inventors are part of a team. Several national contests and programs ask students to work in teams. You might like to work with just one friend or a few friends. You can form a team and ask a teacher to be the coach or the adviser. Sometimes, entire science classes work together as a team.

Teamwork Calls for Cooperation and Compromise

Working with a team is a different experience from working alone. Team members can help one another, divide the work, and also have fun together. Team members can listen to one another's ideas, discuss them, and consider solutions together. Teams work toward a common goal. Elizabeth Hazen and Rachel Brown, inventors in 1948 of the world's first useful antifungal antibiotic, nystatin, both worked for the New York State Department of Health but in different cities. In spite of the distance, they worked as a team, shared the results of tests, and exchanged samples through the U.S. Mail. They donated their royalties—almost $13 million—to academic science.

Inventor's Tip

"Even if you have differences with another person on the team, it really doesn't matter because you're all working toward a common goal."

—*Sarah Friedberg, first-place team, 2003 Christopher Columbus Awards for Now You See It, Now You Don't: Mortality Composting*

The Bath Butler

"What don't you like to do?" teacher Diana Celle asked her son, Kai, who was then a third-grader at Holmes Elementary School in San Diego. He was part of a team participating in the ExploraVision competition. "I don't like getting my bath ready," he said. And so he and his teammates—Sophia Litsey and Meredith Sturmer— set out to research present technology and envision future technology regarding an ordinary bath. They had to illustrate all their ideas on a Web site. With the help of their coach, teacher Kerry McTaggert, and an adult mentor, they started by thinking about what's involved in taking a bath. They went on a field trip to a bath store and found that other than the invention of a soft tub, not many improvements have been made to this ordinary activity. So the kids envisioned the future of bathing. Everyone in the house would use a computer to input instructions about how they'd like their baths—the temperature, the depth, and whether they wanted oils or bubble bath added to the water. In the wall of the bathroom, a mirror would be installed. The mirror would be able to recognize the person, then draw a bath for that individual based on his or her pre-programmed instructions. Afterward, the bather would be dried with warm air coming out of jets installed in a bathroom wall. And that's not all. Check out all of the ideas of this first-place team from the 2002 ExploraVision awards at www.exploravision.org under "Past Winners." "Everyone's ideas made the project better," said Sophia. ∎

Inventor's Tip

"Working as a team gives you more ideas and teaches you that you can't do everything by yourself."

—Meredith Sturmer, first-place team, K–3 division, 2002 ExploraVision for the Bath Butler

Teams can have problems getting along, though, and that can affect a project. Everyone needs to be involved and feel that he or she is part of the team. Everyone needs to know what everyone else is doing. Everyone's ideas need to be heard. Sometimes people don't express their ideas because there isn't time or they are shy about speaking in front of a group. In that case, writing down ideas and using the written comments as the starting point for a brainstorming session can be a good strategy. Someone in the team, a coach, a mentor, or a student, can also take on what can be a rotating job of observing the team dynamic. The aim is to keep everyone working together to achieve the team goal.

Team members should try to agree on how to deal with common group problems. There are ways to handle the problems experienced by most groups. If one of the kids on your team talks too much or tries to be the boss, ask that person to take notes. He or she will be too busy to talk all the time and will also be doing an important job. If some of the kids keep having private conversations during meetings, ask them to share their conversation with the whole group or be quiet if they don't have something important to say. If some kids never say or do anything, ask them to suggest an idea or take on a particular job. If kids arrive late, don't stop the meeting to update them on what has happened. Fill them in later. If your team can't stay on a topic, make a list of things that have to be done, and make sure everyone agrees to stick to it. If everyone starts talking negatively, discuss the work and make sure everyone on your team agrees with the goals and the process. Help everyone to focus on what's going right with the project, instead of on what's gone wrong. If your team is behind schedule, divide the work into smaller units. Set shorter deadlines that will be easier to finish. If kids on your team don't do the jobs they promised to do, ask them if they need help, or have them do other jobs that aren't too important. If some members on your team are fighting, ask them to make the team goal more important than their argument. If that doesn't work, ask a teacher or a coach to mediate the problem. As a last resort, ask them to leave the team.

The need to work out some of these conflicts is an issue for nearly all teams. Paying attention can be hard in any group setting. Yet once people pay attention, they can start to solve problems.

Now You See It, Now You Don't: Mortality Composting

KIDS INVENTING!

"One of the most important things is that you have to compromise on a lot of things," said Carrie Schedler, one member of the eighth-grade team that also included Sarah Friedberg, Emily Roth, and Kathryn Scurci and their coach, science teacher Jon Hood, of Bexley Middle School in Bexley, Ohio. "If we had a fight, we all remembered how much more important this project was to us than our little fight."

The team tackled the problem of the disposal of roadkill. "A lot of people don't take into account that more and more animals are lining the highways, polluting the air, and being buried in the ground, potentially polluting the groundwater," said team member Kathryn Scurci. When the group members started researching the topic, they discovered that the Ohio Department of Transportation burns roadkill, that animal shelters put dead animals in plastic bags and then into landfills, and that farmers often bury 1,000-pound animals they can't eat.

As often happens when inventors research an idea, the students discovered that others had thought about the same problem. When they visited Ohio State University and met with Dr. Harold Keener and his staff at the Agricultural and Research Development Center, they learned about a process called mortality composting, a simple, ecologically safe method of animal disposal using sawdust that had been invented hundreds of years ago. "Mortality composting is very beneficial, but it had been tucked away in a drawer," said team member Emily Roth, "so we wanted to do it and bring it to everyone's attention." Using a formula given to them by Dr. Keener, the students set up boxes filled with mixtures of sawdust, then composted several animals and carefully monitored

Inventor's Tip

"Having the others there boosts you, and it helps you work faster."

—Sarah Friedberg, first-place team, 2003 Christopher Columbus Awards for Now You See It, Now You Don't: Mortality Composting

Members of the Now You See It, Now You Don't team: Carrie Schedler, Kathryn Scurci, Sarah Friedberg, Emily Roth, and coach Jon Hood (left to right).

the process. "This method is clean, odor-free, and quick," said Kathryn. "The animals were completely decomposed. We called it Now You See It, Now You Don't: Mortality Composting." (Check out the project on the team's Web site, www.bexley.k12.oh.us.)

With the results in hand, the team spoke with local officials, state legislators, and the governor, Robert Taft. Articles about their work appeared in the media. "Due to their work, hog and cattle farmers are looking at the idea, and a group in the Philippines is interested in their research," said Jon Hood. The team won first place at the 2003 Christopher Columbus Awards, a national competition that challenges middle school students to explore ways to positively change their communities.

Did teamwork matter? "The project really pulled them together and forced them to rely on each others' strengths. They were able to accomplish phenomenal things," said Jon Hood. ■

"There are few jobs out there where you are a sole, independent worker," said Stephanie Hallman, the competition manager of the Christopher Columbus Awards. "Working with science and technology is basically a discovery process. Brainstorming is a very big part of that. That's why we chose to have the kids work in groups, rather than as individuals."

Small Teams

Teams don't have to be large groups. Two friends can form a team and take advantage of their friendship and their individual areas of interest.

The Big Array System

Peter Alexander Lee, of Carmel, California, was seventeen and a student at the York School when he invited a school friend, Gabe Klapman, then eighteen, of Santa Cruz, California, to join him in doing a project outside of school. "It's fun to do things with someone," said Peter. "And you also get to share the work."

The two friends created a directional hearing aid that they called the Big Array System. It's designed so that sounds occurring in front of a hearing-impaired person are much louder than other sounds in the environment. Why does that matter? Two hearing-impaired friends had explained the problems they experienced with their hearing aids, saying that it was hard to hear a person talking because background sounds were too loud.

"I was interested in the medical aspects," said Gabe. "Peter was interested in engineering and the computer science aspects."

Gabe Klapman (left) and Peter Lee (right) with the model for their Big Array System.

Gabe started by visiting audiologists and people who used hearing aids. He learned that most hearing aids have both a microphone and a small speaker in the earpiece, and they have to be adjusted often. Peter and Gabe designed a hearing aid that wouldn't need constant adjustment. First, they put only the speaker in the earpiece. They used a "big array" of microphones—eight tiny ones arranged on the rim of a hat—and used digital processing technology to process the sound with a computer chip. This allowed them to delay some sounds and add others together. That way, they could allow the sounds from in front of the person to be 7 decibels louder. Sound was relayed to the earpiece by a radio link.

The two students did not have a sophisticated laboratory to work in. They met at Peter's house on weekends and designed their project either at the kitchen table or in the yard when they had problems with reverberations and sound reflecting off the kitchen walls. They admit to advantages and disadvantages of working as a team. "We had to bring each other up to speed and had a little loss of efficiency there," said the teammates. "But what we lost in efficiency in bringing each other up to speed, we gained in the efficiency of combining our efforts," added Gabe.

While others have invented similar systems, no one has used the microphone arrangement as the team did. In 2001, Peter and Gabe placed second in the Team Category at the Intel International Science & Engineering Fair and were finalists in the Siemens Westinghouse Competition in Math, Science & Technology. In 2002, they were inducted into the National Gallery for America's Young Inventors. ∎

Inventor's Tip

"I liked working as a team because we could use our individual talents."

—Gabe Klapman, 2002 Inductee into the National Gallery for America's Young Inventors for the Big Array System

Large Teams

Large teams can divide aspects of the work depending on the skills, capabilities, personalities, and locations of their members.

KIDS INVENTING!

The Littleton InvenTeam

The town of Littleton, New Hampshire, spends approximately $3,000 per winter storm for equipment, materials, and staffing to use salt to clear the snow from Main Street. The salt not only damages the road, it also pollutes the nearby Ammonoosuc River. Highway manager Larry Jackson wanted to heat the sidewalks, a method used by many communities, but it didn't seem that the town could afford to either engineer or operate such a system. In addition, the town was planning a 2005 renovation of Main Street.

Enter thirty-five students from Littleton High School and their physics and robotics teacher, Bill Church. Church wrote a grant proposal with the idea of using the money to invent a system to help with the town's snow-clearing problem. The school was selected as one of three schools to be the inaugural recipients of the Lemelson-MIT InvenTeam Grants; each grant was for $10,000.

Students broke up into small groups to work on various facets of the project: test bed construction, materials testing, heating system mechanics, the solar/wind/hydro components, and the waste heat compression pads. Community employees, school officials, private businesses, and eighteen mentors worked with Church and the students to configure a system of pipes that carried a heated antifreeze solution.

"I loved the feeling of being part of a team," said team member Michelle Doucette. "Being able to sit back and say, 'Hey, I helped come up with that idea!'"

The students' system was installed in new sidewalks at the high school, heated by waste heat from the school's boilers. The installation is being studied by another group of students so that the town can decide whether it can use the system for the Main Street

Check Out What Teams Have Done!

Many team competitions ask teams to investigate solutions to community problems. Check out what student teams have accomplished on the following Web sites:

- www.exploravision.com: ExploraVision is a competition sponsored by Toshiba for students of all interest, skill, and ability levels in grades K through 12 who live in the United States or Canada. It encourages students to explore a vision of a future technology and to research its past and present.

- www.ecybermission.com: eCYBERMISSION is a Web-based science, math, and technology competition for sixth- through ninth-grade teams sponsored by the U.S. Army. It asks students to propose a solution to a real problem in their community, using science, math, and technology.

- www.christophercolumbusawards.com: The Christopher Columbus Awards is a competition for teams of sixth- through eighth-grade students that each work with an adult coach to identify a community issue and use science, technology, and consultations with community leaders and experts to develop an innovative solution.

- www.web.mit.edu/invent/www/inventeam/: InvenTeams is a national Lemelson-MIT Program that provides grants to teams of high school students and their teachers that have submitted proposals for plans to invent something of value for their schools or local communities.

- www.toychallenge.com: TOYchallenge asks teams of kids in grades 5 through 8 to create and design an interactive learning toy or game. The astronaut Sally Ride organized companies and institutions to launch this challenge.

renovation. "They experienced failure and success, and they worked alongside workmen who ply the mechanical trades. They had the benefit of total immersion in a collaborative, high stakes, relevant, and meaningful experience," said George Brodeur, Clerk of the Works, Littleton High School Project. (Check out their project at the Lemelson-MIT Program Web site, www.web.mit.edu/invent/, and search for "InvenTeams.") ■

Inventor's Tip

"One thing I like about working as a team, and also dislike, is how many different views you can get. One person may see a situation differently from someone else on the team. That also sets up room for disagreements about how things should be run. Luckily, some of our 'wouldn't work ideas' turned into 'workable ideas' through compromising. Compromising also allows a little bit of everyone to show through in our final project."

—*Michelle Doucette, Littleton InvenTeam member, 2003*

Activities

1. Brainstorm about Community Concerns

   How can you help your town? Get together with a few friends for an hour and make it fun. Share some snacks, then start throwing out ideas. Think about big and small problems that affect your town. Give yourselves a half-hour to come up with a list of problems, then spend the rest of the hour throwing around ideas for solutions that might involve inventions. All crazy ideas are allowed. In an hour, you just might have an idea for a project or the beginning of one.

2. Plan for Working as a Team

   Think about how you and your friends or classmates could work as a team. How would you

   - Divide the work?
   - Each contribute to the project?
   - Benefit by working as a team?
   - Solve conflicts?

   Check out the types of problems that many teams encounter and the suggested solutions on pages 67–68. Figure out how you would deal with these problems.

7

Learning with a Mentor

Imagine having your own private teacher, someone who guides you as you learn and work on your invention. Someone who gives suggestions if you head in the wrong direction. Someone who sees the possibilities in a failed invention. A person who does all that and more is called a mentor. Many inventors have achieved more with mentors than they might have on their own.

Mentors Are Guides

Mentors can be any age. High school students can be mentors to middle school students. Middle school students can mentor elementary students. Students can also mentor kids of their own age, if they have knowledge to share. Teachers, parents, or relatives can be mentors. Some mentors are older, retired people who have a lot of experience and a fair amount of free time.

Kids who seek out mentors want to learn, and mentors are people who like to help, so both groups benefit. A mentor can communicate with a mentee (the person being mentored) in person, by e-mail, or by phone. A mentor can guide a student for a few hours, for one day, for a few weeks, or even for years.

While a teacher works with a class, mentors work with one or more people at a time to help them learn a skill or achieve a goal. Many parents seek out mentors for their kids. Some schools match

Inventor's Tip

"There are many, many professors, teachers, and professionals who would be delighted to help you find and develop ideas, understand key concepts, or even get access to sophisticated equipment. You just need to have a plan and ask them."

—Peter Lee, 2002 inductee into the National Gallery for America's Young Inventors for the Big Array System students with mentors. Often, community groups or organizations also arrange mentor relationships.

Many people work with one mentor on one project and with another mentor on a different project. Sometimes, a mentor and a student work together for a while, but then the mentor no longer has free time to spare or the student doesn't feel that he or she is learning anything new. If this happens, or if the relationship doesn't work out for any other reason, the student can seek out another mentor.

Every mentor relationship is different, depending on the people involved. You and your mentor will work out your own relationship, but here are some stories about other students and their mentors.

The American Sign Language Translator

When Ryan Patterson of Colorado was four years old, he went to Disneyland with his parents. After riding on "It's a Small World" three times, he begged his parents to go on it again. "What an unusual fascination he has with these dolls," commented his mother, Sherry Patterson, to his dad, Randy, as they boarded the ride again. This time, she watched him. While Ryan's sister, Kim, was looking at the dolls, Ryan's face was turned upward. "He was looking at the wiring," said Mrs. Patterson. At home, Ryan loved to take the appliances apart and put them back together. He loved electricity. At age six, his favorite toy was an extension cord. When he was in second grade, he wired a floor mop so that it would spin by itself. "He hated mopping the floor," she said. "That was one of his chores."

Ryan asked questions all the time, of his parents and then of his teachers. By the time he was in third grade, he had so many questions that his teacher suggested he work with a mentor. When Ryan's mother called John McConnell, a retired physicist with a strong background in electronics who had worked at Los Alamos National Laboratory, he was surprised to be asked to mentor such a young boy. He agreed to talk to Ryan and was impressed by the boy's curiosity and focus. They started by working together on Saturdays, at first for an hour and then all day. They continued to meet every Saturday for the next nine years.

"At Mr. and Mrs. McConnell's house," said Ryan, "they had a shop where I could work on electronic projects." And work, he did. In a fourth-grade contest to decorate Valentine's Day boxes, Ryan created an electronic box shaped like a windmill, which included a voice chip. "He'd learned enough electronics by then," said McConnell. If you dropped an envelope into the windmill, the valentine passed by a micro-switch and started the action. Lights went on, the windmill blades turned, and a recording of Ryan's voice said, "Thank you. Have a Happy Valentine's Day."

"I created my first actual 'invention' in seventh grade," said Ryan. He was motivated to do the work when his mother heard several news reports about the effects of electromagnetic fields from power lines and expressed her concern about whether the cords to all the electronic devices in his bedroom might be harmful. He measured the fields and the effect of the position of the wires, and his tests proved that the cords were safe. What he'd invented was a device that could detect AC power lines in the walls of buildings. "Now such a device is on the market, but nothing like it existed at the time, so I received an award for it," said Ryan.

John McConnell guided Ryan's exploration. He provided information and answered his questions about semiconductors, integrated circuits, analog and digital circuitry, and more.

"He was always very focused," said McConnell. In tenth grade, Ryan built a high-speed, low-cost search robot that could be controlled from a remote location so that humans wouldn't be in danger when searching an area. It had head sensors, sonar, and a video camera equipped with night vision so that it could operate in the dark. At the Intel International Science and Engineering Fair, Ryan won Best of Engineering Category for the robot.

When he was seventeen years old, Ryan invented the American Sign Language Finger-Spelling Translator—a golf glove that translates American Sign Language (ASL) into letters that can be read on a small screen. Ryan got the idea for the translator while at Burger King, when he noticed that several deaf teenagers needed a friend to place their order. Teenagers should be more independent, he thought.

He wired a golf glove with ten sensors, a small circuit board containing a micro-controller, an analog-to-digital converter, and a radio-frequency transmitter. When he put the glove on and signed, the sensors read the signs and wirelessly transmitted and translated the letters to a display module—a screen that he could hold in his other hand. *Time* magazine listed the American Sign Translator as one of the "Coolest Inventions of 2002."

Ryan acknowledges that having a mentor made a big difference. "Without the knowledge Mr. McConnell has given me," said Ryan, "there is no way I could have successfully created the translator. The mentor-protégé relationship had a bigger impact on me than anything else in my life." Ryan not

Ryan Patterson and his mentor John McConnell at the 2001 Intel ISEF Awards.

only won first place in the engineering category at the Intel International Science and Engineering Fair in 2001 for the glove, he also won the Intel Young Scientist Award—the highest award given to the fourteen hundred competing students—and he won the Glenn Seaborg Award, which granted him a trip to the Nobel Prize Awards in Stockholm, Sweden. In addition, he won first place in the Siemens Westinghouse Competition in Math, Science & Technology in 2001, an award that included a $100,000 college scholarship. In 2002, he won the Intel Science Talent Search (often called the junior Nobel Prize). When asked what she thought her son would do with the rest of his life, Mrs. Patterson said, "I think he'll invent more things to help people. That's what he's always done." ■

School Mentor Programs

Many schools and school districts are enthusiastic about the importance of mentors. While John McConnell mentored Ryan, he was also a mentor to other kids. He often visited schools in Ryan's school district and presented science demonstrations. Eventually, the district (Mesa County School District 51) provided him with 5,000 square feet in one of its buildings where he set up and still leads the Western Colorado Math and Science Center. This learning center is open to the public and has more than 160 hands-on displays related to math and science. "Having the kids play with the displays is a way to mentor thousands," said McConnell. You can visit the science center's Web site at www.sithok.org.

Hathaway Brown School in Shaker Heights, Ohio, has a motto: "We learn not for school but for life." The motto might describe its Student Research Program as well. Patricia Hunt, a former scientific researcher and now the director of the Student Research Program at Hathaway Brown, brainstormed in 1998 with Head of School William Christ to design an afterschool and summertime multiyear program. High school students begin the program by talking to Hunt about their interests. Hunt eventually places them under the mentorship of a variety of scientists, medical researchers, and other professionals at nearby research institutions, including Cleveland Clinic Foundation, University Hospitals, Case Western Reserve University (CWRU), Case Western Reserve University School of Medicine, Cleveland Museum of Natural History, Cleveland Museum of Art, and NASA Glenn Research Center. Although at first students perform routine tasks, almost all of them go on to accomplish their own projects with the help of the mentors.

The Chlorine Sensor

Bonnie Gurry, of Hathaway Brown, worked with Dr. Chung Chiun Liu at the Electronic Design Center at Case Western Reserve University during all four years of high school. "Dr. Liu offered me the chance to create my own sensor, but I had to choose what it would detect," said Bonnie. "Since my swim team's practice was canceled when we discovered that the chlorine levels were too high, I decided to design a sensor to monitor the chlorine levels in a pool. I learned a lot in the process, especially that you don't succeed overnight. I realize now that a project can be done in steps. I've gotten a taste of life at the professional level, and I'm still in high school." Bonnie, Dr. Liu, and others who worked on the project gained a patent for the sensor in 2004. ■

Each year, more than a hundred students participate in the Hathaway Brown program. Students' work has been cited in almost a hundred scientific publications, and students' names are included on two patent applications. Two students have gained patents. An extension of the program, the Outreach Student Research Program, started in 1999, teamed Cleveland Public Schools minority students with mentors at the same institutions. Students also received stipends for their work. After the program was running for a few years, Case Western Reserve School of Medicine took an interest in it and asked Hathaway Brown to partner with the School of Medicine in expanding the Outreach portion of the program as a joint venture. More students now take advantage of it, and many cities are starting similar programs.

Inventor's Tip

"For a mentor, I looked for somebody who could commit some time and wanted me to succeed. I had one mentor. Although I wanted to learn about electronics and my mentor was a physicist, he knew more than I did, and he knew where to find other information. Other students should keep in mind that only one person may ever come around and offer to be a mentor."

—Ryan Patterson, inventor of the American Sign Language Translator; first place, 2001 Siemens Westinghouse Competition in Math, Science & Technology; winner, 2002 Intel Science Talent Search; winner, 2002 Glenn Seaborg Award (which included a trip to the Nobel Prize Awards)

Mentors from the Business Community

Sometimes students and their parents seek out mentors in the business community. Students can learn not only about inventing but also about the business world. They acquire skills, such as how to use different kinds of machinery or software programs, and also learn how and whether their ideas for inventions might become products sold in stores. Mentors can help young inventors explore these possibilities.

The Ice Crawler

"When they came, they had all the intelligence, drive, and motivation that you could ask for. What they did not have was a facility, the infrastructure of an electronics lab and a machine shop that we have in our business," said John Pursley, the president of Envision Product Design, a robotics company. He was a mentor to Heather and Hanna Craig, twins from Anchorage, Alaska, during their last two years at East High School.

Hanna and Heather's parents wanted the twins to have a mentor. "When they entered high school, we thought the greatest way for them to expand their interests was through the mentorship program offered at their school," said their mom, Carol Hult. Their father, Paul Craig, contacted Pursley.

"We knew we wanted to invent something to do with Alaska," said Heather and Hanna, who had worked on many science fair projects throughout their childhood.

"Everybody gets ideas," said Pursley, "but there's a series of questions you ask about ideas before you can decide whether to spend effort and resources. That's the process I wanted them to get a feel for." One of their first ideas was to make an avalanche rescue tool. "I pointed out that many items for avalanche rescue already existed," he said. "Part of what I saw as my job was to fill them in on how to look at the market, to see what areas weren't being addressed." Three months of brainstorming led the twins to come up with the idea of an ice-crawling rescue device.

Picture the scene. Two friends are walking on a frozen pond. The ice cracks, and one of them falls in the icy water. In trying to rescue the friend, the other friend falls in. A rescue crew goes out on the pond to help them, but they fall in the icy water as well. The pond won't support a car or other rescue devices. How can the people be rescued? It's a real-life problem. As their mentor pointed out to the twins, few products have been created for this type of rescue. Over the next year and a half, Heather and Hanna spent six hours a week at Envision Product Design. Half the time they helped out the

Heather (left) and Hanna Craig, ready to demonstrate the Ice Crawler.

company doing everything from sweeping the floors to soldering wires and building cable; the rest of the time they spent on their project.

The result was a prototype of the Ice Crawler, a 4-foot-long robot that can crawl on the ice and over rocks in areas that are hard for humans and animals to get to. It is light-weight and can be folded up and carried by rescue teams. A tether is attached to the crawler. Wiring inside the tether links the crawler to a control panel that Hanna and Heather would use when testing to guide the crawler and turn it on and off. In a rescue situation, when the crawler would come within reach of a person, he or she could grab onto the tether and be pulled to safety. Hanna and Heather used a 30-foot tether for their prototype, which allowed them or any rescue team to be a safe distance from the person in trouble. The girls also put a video camera on the front of the robot so that they could see where it was going. The crawler was powered by two 12-volt drive motors—actually, car window motors that the twins salvaged from a junkyard. They used old bicycle sprockets to pull the track system and keep the track in place. All in all, the prototype cost less than $500 to make.

Mentoring Resources on the Internet

These Web sites give information on how to find a mentor, and some will assist in matching you with a qualified person.

- www.sciencebuddies.com: Science Buddies is an online program. It is a nonprofit organization that matches students with mentors and advisers to help youths improve their science skills. Anyone can pose a question on the "Ask an Expert" online bulletin board. One-on-one e-mentoring with limited enrollment is also offered.
- www.mentors.ca: This Canadian site has "yellow pages" of mentor services and offers many tips on getting a mentor.
- www.mentoring.org: MENTOR/National Mentoring Partnership was created in 1990 by the financiers and philanthropists Geoff Boisi and Ray Chambers, with the goal of connecting America's young people with caring adult mentors. Their Web site provides help for arranging mentor relationships in more than twenty states.
- www.amazing-kids.org/mentors.html: The Amazing Kids!—Amazing Mentors! section of the Amazing Kids! Web site acts as a "mentoring hub," providing resources and connections for mentors and prospective mentors who are interested in mentoring children. The Amazing Kids!—Amazing Mentors! outreach program works closely with schools, businesses, and the community to coordinate and implement a mentoring program within each community, through the Amazing Kids! Centers.
- www.acementor.org: The ACE Mentor Program is for high school students who are exploring careers in architecture, construction, or engineering. The mentors are professionals from design and construction firms who volunteer their time and energy to meet regularly with students to acquaint them with the three disciplines.

"It was a slow process of improving it until it worked effectively," said Heather. "Everytime we added something or finished it, we tested it. Usually, it wouldn't work. It had a lot to do with refining, a lot of redesigning, changing materials."

"We couldn't have done this whole project without John," said both Heather and Hanna. "He was an invaluable resource." Hanna and Heather won second place and a $50,000 college scholarship in the team category of the Siemens Westinghouse Competition in Math, Science & Technology in 2001. They were granted Patent No. 6,837,318B1 for the Ice Crawler on January 4, 2005. ∎

To find a mentor, talk to your teachers, parents, librarians, or relatives and let them know what kind of mentor you're looking for. Check with local businesses, clubs, or organizations, such as the Chamber of Commerce, to find out if they have mentor programs. You can also try various online sources (see the box on page 80).

Inventor's Tip

"Importance of a mentor? They have a more thorough knowledge than we do in some cases, and without that knowledge we can't succeed. They can help us if we're going off track or going in the wrong direction."

—Harris Sokoloff, 2001 inductee into the National Gallery for America's Young Inventors for HEADS UP

Activities

1. What Would You Like to Learn from a Mentor?

   Ask yourself what you could learn from a mentor that would help you make an invention. What tools do you want to learn to operate? Do you need to know how to conduct an experiment? Here are some other topics that you might work on with a mentor: woodworking, electronics, rocketry, sewing, construction, computer skills, and engineering.

2. Ask a Mentor Some Questions

   Make up a list of questions that you would ask a potential mentor, such as

   a. Why did you decide to become a mentor?

   b. What area of knowledge do you have to share with kids?

   c. How much time do you have to spend as a mentor?

   d. How would you organize our time together? Where would we work?

   f. What would you like the outcome of our mentor relationship to be?

8

Patenting an Invention

Once you have finished an invention, applying for a patent is an option. Patents describe exactly how an invention is made or works. If you are granted a patent, you gain the right to own your idea. Patents give an inventor the right to be the only person who can make, sell, or use an invention for a period of time—up to twenty years in the United States. An invention is defined by the United States Patent and Trademark Office as new, useful, and unobvious—something that not just anyone would think of. Many of the patents granted long ago were for inventions that are now an important part of our lives. In the beginning, though, the inventor protected the new idea with a patent.

- Alexander Graham Bell gained Patent No. 174,465 for the Electric Speakers Telephone in 1876.
- Mary Anderson gained Patent No. 743,891 for the Window Cleaning Device (the Windshield Wiper) in 1903.
- Percy L. Spencer gained Patent No. 2,408,235 for the High Efficiency Magnetron (the Microwave Oven) in 1946.

How Inventions Are Patented

Governments grant patents to inventors. Canada, England, France, Germany, Japan, and most other countries around the world have patent systems. On April 10, 1790, President George Washington signed the bill that laid the foundations of the modern American patent system. Since then, almost 7 million patents have been granted in the United States. More than three thousand new patents are issued every week. Each patent is given a number that you can see printed on common products like toys or tools or on the backs of packages.

Patents stop other people from making, selling, or using the patent holder's inventions. Patents are a government's way of giving inventors a head start. An inventor can start a business based on his or her idea or can sell or license the idea to a company that will make or sell a product based on the invention. When the term of a patent is over, others can make or use that invention.

Patents aren't cheap. Applying for a patent can cost a minimum of $4,000 in fees, and that is without using a lawyer. Fees for patents vary, depending on the details, so some patents may cost more than others. Although they are costly, patents can be valuable to inventors. A patent is property. It can be used as the basis of a business, or the right to use the idea can be sold to someone else.

When you get an idea for an invention, you can work on it for as long as you like. Once you begin to sell it or announce it publicly, however, which includes presenting it at a science or an invention fair, you must apply for a patent within one year, or you could lose your right to the invention.

> **Inventor's Tip**
>
> "Don't be intimidated by the process of getting a patent. If you want to go for it, don't worry about what others may say. Don't let them influence how far you can go."
>
> —*Akhil Rastogi, gained a patent for the E-Z Gallon*

The Patent Search

If you want to patent an invention, where do you start? When you first came up with your idea, you did research to prove that it was an invention. Perhaps you looked through magazines and catalogues or on Web sites that deal with the same topic as your idea. Or you interviewed a store owner to ask whether anything like your invention exists. There is one more thing you can do: conduct a patent search.

The U.S. Patent and Trademark Office in Alexandria, Virginia, contains 29 million documents in twenty miles of file cabinets—all patents. Don't worry, you don't have to look through every one of them. You don't even have to go to Virginia. You can visit any of the eighty-six patent and trademark depository libraries around the United States. (Check for one near you at www.uspto.gov.) Or you can do a patent search online at the same Web site. Patents granted since 1976 can be searched online by name, number, or topic. Patents issued prior to that can only be searched by using the patent number or the classification number.

Check out these Web sites for more instructions on patent searching:

- www.about.com has a lot of information about inventing and includes a section called Patent Searching for Young Inventors. To access the page, go to the site and type "young inventors" in the search box. A list will appear that includes the page Patent Searching for Young Inventors.
- www.uspto.gov/go/kids is the Kids' Pages section of the U.S. Patent and Trademark Office. The Web site offers many tips on doing a patent search. Check out the section for kids ages six through twelve to find a link about patent searches.

Doing a patent search online is free, fun, and interesting. You might discover in your research that nobody else has a patent on an idea like yours. But doing the job of searching patents can be difficult, especially if you don't know exactly how to look. You may find patents that are a bit like your idea, but not be able to determine if they are similar enough to keep you from patenting your idea. Evaluating patents can be confusing. Many people hire a lawyer or a patent agent to do a patent search. Yet, you can give a lawyer or a patent agent the information you've already discovered to save the time and money it would take him or her to do the same research.

How to Do a Patent Search

Go to the U.S. Patent and Trademark Office Web site (www.uspto.gov). You are at the USPTO home page. You can look for patents in three ways: by number, by name, or by using search words.

Patent Search by Number

Patent numbers are printed on common products like toys or tools, on packages, or in literature that comes with a product. Try looking for one. Here's an example: Patent No. 5,865,438.

To Search:

1. On the home page, look on the left for Patents and click on Search.
2. You're on a new page. Under Issued Patents, click on Patent Number Search.
3. In the space under Query, type in Patent No. 5,865,438 (or any other number). Click on Search to continue.
4. The patent or a list of patents will appear. Look at the patent and click on Images to see the drawings. (If a list of patents appears, read the descriptions and click on the one you want to see.)

Patent Search by Name

You can search by the inventor's name only for things that have been invented since 1976. Pick some of the kid inventors listed in this book, type in their names, and check out their patents. (Try Akhil Rastogi, Jonathan Fleck, Abigail Fleck, Christina Adams, Kavita Shukla, or Ole Andersen.)

To Search:

1. On the home page, look on the left for Patents and click on Search.

2. You're on a new page. Under Issued Patents, click on Quick Search.

3. In the space for Term 1, type in the name of an inventor (last name, first name) who has been granted a patent since 1976. Click on Search to continue.

4. The patent or a list of patents will appear. Look at the patent and click on Images to see the drawings. (If a list of patents appears, read the descriptions and click on the one you want to see.)

Patent Search by Using Search Words

This is the best way to look through patents to see if any of them are like your invention. You can type in a word or a combination of words. For example, you could type in "skate-boards," "action figures," or "bicycles." A list will appear of all the patents that relate to those words.

To Search:

1. On the home page, look on the left for Patents and click on Search.

2. You're on a new page. Under Issued Patents, click on Quick Search.

3. In the space for Term 1, type in the words for your search. Click on Search to continue.

4. Look through the list of patent numbers and titles. Do any of them seem like yours? If so, click on the number or the title to view it.

5. When you find a patent that is similar to yours, look at the section in the patent called References Cited. That is a list of similar or related patents. Look up those patents by number (if the patent was granted before 1976) or click on the patent number to the left (if the patent was granted after 1976) to find out more about inventions that may be like your idea.

Types of Patents

There are three types of patents: utility, plant, and design patents. Most patents are utility patents. They are granted for machines with moving parts, for items that don't have moving parts, or for a process. Utility patents last for twenty years from the date that the inventor applies for the patent. Page 86 shows an example of a utility patent for an invention with no moving parts.

The Crayon Holder

Cassidy Goldstein was granted utility Patent No. 6,402,407 for a crayon holder that makes it easier for you to draw with a crayon. "I was always the type of kid who never threw anything away, thinking that I would find some creative use for it," said Cassidy. Once while she was a student at Scarsdale Middle School in Scarsdale, New York, she found a plastic tube with a plastic top and kept it. Later, she stuck a piece of crayon in the top. Presto! A crayon holder. That was the quick part. It took six years for the patent and the manufacturing process. "To see it in the stores is just amazing," said Cassidy. ■

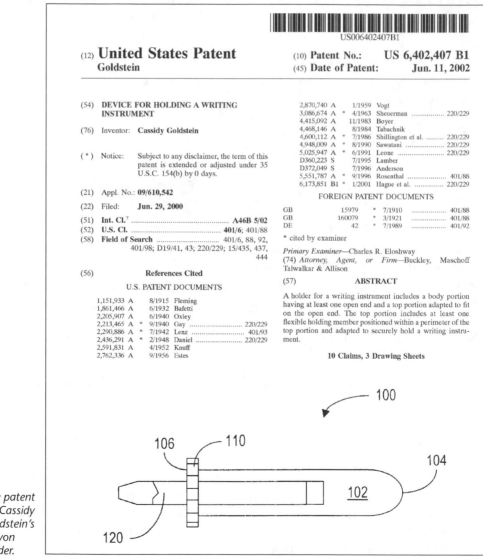

US006402407B1

(12) **United States Patent**
Goldstein

(10) Patent No.: **US 6,402,407 B1**
(45) Date of Patent: **Jun. 11, 2002**

(54) **DEVICE FOR HOLDING A WRITING INSTRUMENT**

(76) Inventor: **Cassidy Goldstein**

(*) Notice: Subject to any disclaimer, the term of this patent is extended or adjusted under 35 U.S.C. 154(b) by 0 days.

(21) Appl. No.: **09/610,542**

(22) Filed: **Jun. 29, 2000**

(51) Int. Cl.[7] **A46B 5/02**
(52) U.S. Cl. **401/6**; 401/88
(58) Field of Search 401/6, 88, 92, 401/98; D19/41, 43; 220/229; 15/435, 437, 444

(56) **References Cited**

U.S. PATENT DOCUMENTS

1,151,933 A		8/1915	Fleming	
1,861,466 A		6/1932	Bafetti	
2,205,907 A		6/1940	Oxley	
2,213,465 A	*	9/1940	Gay	220/229
2,290,886 A	*	7/1942	Lenz	401/93
2,436,291 A	*	2/1948	Daniel	220/229
2,591,831 A		4/1952	Knuff	
2,762,336 A		9/1956	Estes	

2,870,740 A		1/1959	Vogt	
3,086,674 A	*	4/1963	Sheuerman	220/229
4,415,092 A		11/1983	Boyer	
4,468,146 A		8/1984	Tabachnik	
4,600,112 A	*	7/1986	Shillington et al.	220/229
4,948,009 A	*	8/1990	Sawatani	220/229
5,025,947 A	*	6/1991	Leone	220/229
D360,223 S		7/1995	Lamber	
D372,049 S		7/1996	Anderson	
5,551,787 A	*	9/1996	Rosenthal	401/88
6,173,851 B1	*	1/2001	Hague et al.	220/229

FOREIGN PATENT DOCUMENTS

GB	15979	*	7/1910	401/88
GB	160079	*	3/1921	401/88
DE	42	*	7/1989	401/92

* cited by examiner

Primary Examiner—Charles R. Eloshway
(74) *Attorney, Agent, or Firm*—Buckley, Maschoff Talwalkar & Allison

(57) **ABSTRACT**

A holder for a writing instrument includes a body portion having at least one open end and a top portion adapted to fit on the open end. The top portion includes at least one flexible holding member positioned within a perimeter of the top portion and adapted to securely hold a writing instrument.

10 Claims, 3 Drawing Sheets

The patent for Cassidy Goldstein's crayon holder.

A skateboarding teen inventor received a patent for an invention with moving parts: shock absorbers for skateboards.

O-Shock

"I did a little ollie off the stairs, and my foot came off the front of the board and landed in a weird spot, and I snapped three tendons in my foot," said Ole Andersen, of Camino, California, then in his early teens. While he was recuperating, Ole, a hands-on kid, was working in his dad's garage workshop, trying to put springs on the

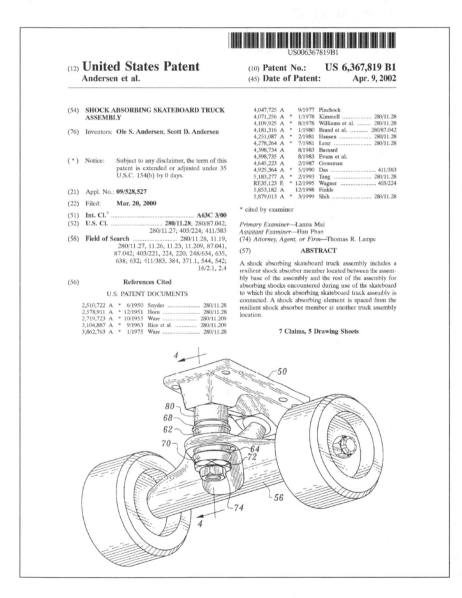

The patent for Ole Andersen's O-Shock device.

skateboard assembly. His mom and dad walked by. "I wouldn't have broken my foot if I'd had suspension on my skateboard trucks, " he told them. Ole's dad, Scott Andersen, thought that was a great idea. "Skateboarders feel a constant vibration as they ride on pavement for hours," he said. "Their knees get sore." So Ole's dad helped him work on his idea. Ole designed a suspension unit to dampen the vibration and gained utility Patent No.6,474,666 for the Shock Absorbing Skate Truck Assembly. O-Shock has since been produced commercially, and skateboarders who use it are riding a little easier. Check it out at www.oshock.com. ■

Plant patents are granted for new varieties of plants—apples, daisies, strawberries, plums, geraniums, roses, and so on. The patents last for twenty years.

Design patents are granted for new designs. They last for a period of fourteen years. If you come up with a new design—say, for a clock that looks like a spaceship—you would apply for a design patent. The patent would be only for the design—for the way the clock looks, not for the way it works. Design patents can be granted for chairs, for cars, for a type of clothing, and even for milk spouts.

KIDS INVENTING!

The E-Z Gallon

Akhil Rastogi, of Fairfax, Virginia, had been trying to help his mom, Deepa Aggarwal, who had nerve damage in her hand. She was taking care of a new-born baby and relied on Akhil for help. One problem was that he usually spilled milk all over the table when trying to pour it. "Every time it was from a full gallon, it would always spill everywhere," said Akhil. His mother gave him advice, like, "Hold it with two hands," or "Lift it higher," but nothing worked.

So Akhil used modeling clay to make a spout that would fit on the mouth of the milk jug. With that in place, he could tilt the jug, and milk would flow out of the spout and into a glass. He called it the E-Z Gallon. It helped his mom and won him first place in his age group in the 1988 Invent America! Student Invention Contest at Olde Creek Elementary School in Fairfax County, Virginia, and first place again in Invent America's state competition in Virginia that same year. He was just seven years old at the time.

Contest judges suggested that he think about getting a patent for his idea. "I didn't even know what a patent was," said Akhil, but he told his parents. Akhil and his dad did a patent search. "It was kind of daunting," admitted Akhil. "Usually, the standard way to go about it is to have a patent lawyer do a search for you, but we chose to do it ourselves. We went to the patent office file room where they keep patents on inventions like mine and spent a lot of hours looking through the files.

Inventor's Tip

"Make sure a patent or a marketing company is trustworthy. There are many companies that promise to take your invention and make you rich but disappear and steal your idea."

—*Austin Meggitt, a 1999 inductee into the National Gallery for America's Young Inventors, gained a patent for the Glove and Battie Caddie*

In the end, we didn't find anything similar enough to the spout. We went ahead and filed an application for a patent. Even that was an ordeal," he admitted. "There are all these rules and regulations. You have to have drawings of a certain size and in a certain ink, but we finally got it done." At age eleven, Akhil was issued design Patent No. 329,810 in 1992 for "Pouring Spout for a Disposable Liquid Container." "At first, I didn't see it as anything that serious," said Akhil, "because it was such a simple invention. Once we started getting serious about it, it dawned on me that simple didn't mean not good. It was simple, but it served a purpose."

Akhil and his family paid to have a plastic prototype made of his spout but decided

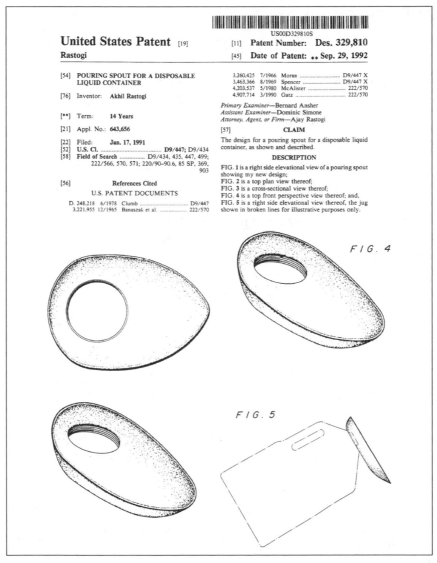

The patent for Akhil Rastogi's E-Z Gallon.

against making it as a product. "The estimates were way out of our league," said Akhil, "so we left it at that. It was fun."

Akhil's E-Z Gallon did not become a product sold in stores. That doesn't mean it wasn't important to him. When he was twelve, the Intellectual Property Owners, Inc., an association representing patent, trademark, and copyright owners, honored Akhil. "It was nice to use my ingenuity to help my mom," said Akhil, who later graduated from James Madison University and then went on to University of Virginia Medical School. "As a result, I was able to have an internship at the National Institutes of Health (NIH) during the summer of 1999. And in the end it helped me get into medical school. It opened a lot of doors." ■

Patent Applications

In a patent application, an inventor is asked to list his or her name and address and then answer questions, such as

- What is your invention and how does it work?
- How is your invention better than and different from others?
- What is the name of your invention?
- What inventions like yours have received patents?
- What is the name of your patent attorney or agent if you have one?

You also have to provide three-dimensional drawings of your invention and you have to write a "claim." A claim is a careful description of exactly what makes one invention different from every other invention. Since the claim defines what makes the idea an invention, it is an important part of the application. Claims for design patents can be quite simple, since they refer back to the design to explain how the item is new. For example, on Akhil Rastogi's design patent for the E-Z Gallon, the claim is "The design for a pouring spout for a disposable liquid container, as shown and described." (See the patent on page 89.)

Claims for utility patents can be more complicated. They describe the exact way that an invention is built or works. When he was ten, Rich Stachowski invented the Underwater Walkie-Talkie. Rich had been snorkeling in Hawaii with his dad and was frustrated not to be able to talk to him. In 1999, Rich gained Patent No. 5,877,460 for a "device for talking underwater." The utility patent included thirteen claims. The first one says:

> What is claimed is: 1. A device for talking underwater, said device comprising: a) a body having a small opening and a large opening; b) a thin diaphragm covering said large opening; c) a mouth fitting surrounding said small opening; d) at least one one-way blow valve mounted in a wall of said body for allowing exhaled air to escape, wherein said blow valve releases air in the form of bubbles having a diameter less than 5 millimeters; whereby speaking into said small opening through mouth fitting couples sound waves to surrounding water through said diaphragm.

You can see that the first claim describes the device in detail. The other claims include details about sizes and materials—for example, "said small holes are approximately 0.1 to 0.15 inch in diameter." Rich's Underwater Walkie-Talkies were produced and sold in Target and other stores. Patents like Rich's include many details, either drawn or stated, which describe exactly how an invention is unique. After reading a patent, someone else could make the invention. And when the patent expires, anyone can do just that.

If you submit an application for a patent, you'll receive a notice saying that the U.S. Patent and Trademark Office received your application. Then, patent examiners review the applications and do their own patent searches to discover whether the ideas are inventions—that is, are they new, useful, and unobvious? This process can take up to a year and a half. Many patent applications are granted, but many are also turned down for a variety of reasons. If there's a fundamental problem with the application, it can be turned down. That is another reason people hire patent attorneys: to review or write their applications.

If you are granted a patent, you have the exclusive right to your invention for a period of time and can either make a product based on the invention or not. You could also license or grant use of the patent to a company or companies interested in making your invention into a product. Nobody else can make, use, sell, or import the patented invention in the United States without your permission. Some inventions, however, never become products.

Patent Infringement

Sometimes people do use a patented invention without permission. This is called patent infringement. It is the responsibility of the patent holder to defend his or her patent, but doing that can be costly. You have to send letters telling whoever is using your invention or idea to stop, and you may have to hire a patent attorney to take action against the person or the company that is infringing on your patent.

KIDS INVENTING!

Makin' Bacon

Abbey Fleck, of Birchwood, Minnesota, was eight years old when she invented a dish for cooking bacon in the microwave. Her dad was cooking bacon one day and he used paper towels to soak up the excess bacon grease. Then he ran out of towels. Abbey thought, Why not drape bacon strips over a rack, pop it into the microwave, and let the bacon grease drip onto the tray? Bingo! The Flecks got a patent, formed a company, registered their trademark Makin' Bacon, and have sold millions of their Makin' Bacon dishes since 1994.

After Makin' Bacon was on the market for a few years, another company started to sell a similar product. The Flecks went to court to protect their invention. The other company agreed to stop making its product, one they called the Incredible Bacon Cooker, paid Abbey and her dad over a hundred thousand dollars, and agreed to send the Flecks the molds it used to make its product. Makin' Bacon continues to sell. ■

KIDS INVENTING!

Calibrated Angle and Depth Scissors

Ariel Krasik-Geiger was always interested in math and science. He loved to work with tools, and by the time he was nine he could use not only a screwdriver and a hammer but also a chop saw, a drill, a drill press, and a lathe. "My dad is an inventor,

---

How to Look at a Patent

Note the numbers next to the items on Ariel's patent (on the next page). Those items are included on all patents. If you can read Ariel's patent, you can read any patent.

1. Last name of the inventor.

2. Number of the patent.

3. Date the patent was granted.

4. Name of the invention.

5. Name and address of the inventor(s)

6. Term: how long a patent lasts. Some patent terms may be extended or adjusted because of certain delays during the application process. (The twenty-year term of this utility patent was extended by 361 days.)

7. Application number.

8. Date the application was filed.

9. U.S. Classification: all inventions are organized into classes and subclasses. This gives the class (30) and the subclass (233).

10. Field of Search: other patents that the invention is based on or that are similar.

11. References Cited: patents that are most like the invention and why.

12. Primary Examiner: the person at the U.S. Patent and Trademark Office who evaluated the patent application.

13. Attorney, Agent, or Firm: the inventor or a person or a company that represents the inventor.

14. Abstract: a description and explanation of the invention.

(continued)

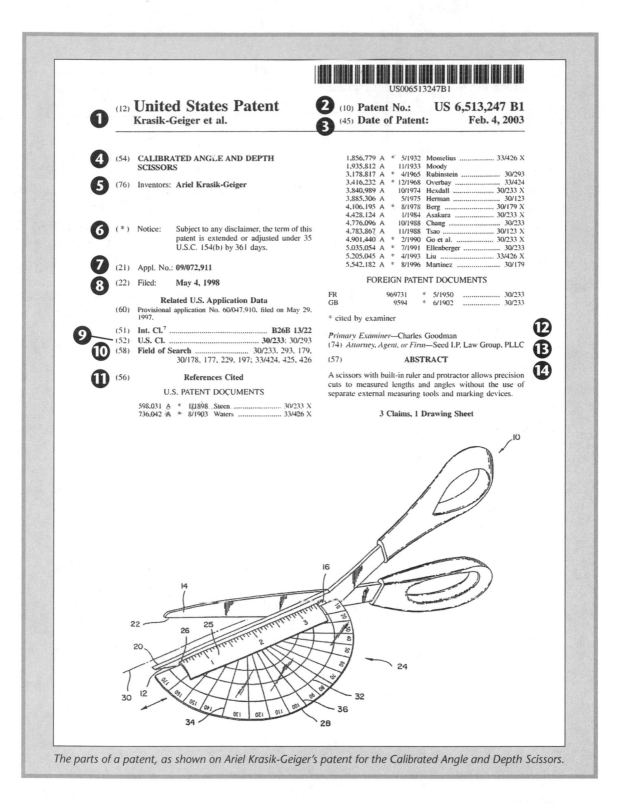

(1) (12) **United States Patent**
Krasik-Geiger et al.

US006513247B1

(2) (10) **Patent No.:** US 6,513,247 B1
(3) (45) **Date of Patent:** Feb. 4, 2003

(4) (54) CALIBRATED ANGLE AND DEPTH SCISSORS

(5) (76) Inventors: **Ariel Krasik-Geiger**

(6) (*) Notice: Subject to any disclaimer, the term of this patent is extended or adjusted under 35 U.S.C. 154(b) by 361 days.

(7) (21) Appl. No.: **09/072,911**

(8) (22) Filed: **May 4, 1998**

Related U.S. Application Data
(60) Provisional application No. 60/047,910, filed on May 29, 1997.

(9) (51) Int. Cl.[7] B26B 13/22
(10) (52) U.S. Cl. 30/233; 30/293
(58) Field of Search 30/233, 293, 179, 30/178, 177, 229, 197; 33/424, 425, 426

(11) (56) **References Cited**

U.S. PATENT DOCUMENTS

598,031 A	*	1/1898	Steen	30/233 X
736,042 A	*	8/1903	Waters	33/426 X
1,856,779 A	*	5/1932	Montelius	33/426 X
1,935,812 A		11/1933	Moody	
3,178,817 A	*	4/1965	Rubinstein	30/293
3,416,232 A	*	12/1968	Overbay	33/424
3,840,989 A		10/1974	Hexdall	30/233 X
3,885,306 A		5/1975	Herman	30/123
4,106,195 A	*	8/1978	Berg	30/179 X
4,428,124 A		1/1984	Asakura	30/233 X
4,776,096 A		10/1988	Chang	30/233
4,783,867 A		11/1988	Tsao	30/123 X
4,901,440 A	*	2/1990	Go et al.	30/233 X
5,035,054 A	*	7/1991	Ellenberger	30/233
5,205,045 A	*	4/1993	Liu	33/426 X
5,542,182 A	*	8/1996	Martinez	30/179

FOREIGN PATENT DOCUMENTS

FR	969731	*	5/1950	30/233
GB	9594	*	6/1902	30/233

* cited by examiner

(12) *Primary Examiner*—Charles Goodman
(13) (74) *Attorney, Agent, or Firm*—Seed I.P. Law Group, PLLC

(14) (57) **ABSTRACT**

A scissors with built-in ruler and protractor allows precision cuts to measured lengths and angles without the use of separate external measuring tools and marking devices.

3 Claims, 1 Drawing Sheet

The parts of a patent, as shown on Ariel Krasik-Geiger's patent for the Calibrated Angle and Depth Scissors.

and we have a full workshop downstairs," said Ariel. "I was always using my hands with mechanical stuff."

At age ten he had the idea for a pair of scissors with a ruler on it. "I thought you could easily attach a ruler to the edge of a blade," he said. The idea was to be able to cut into a piece of paper at a certain depth (one, two, or three inches, for example). "The first prototype was a cutout of cardboard attached with simple brass rivets. Nothing fancy," said Ariel.

"When I read about the Craftsman/NSTA Young Inventors Awards Program, I got interested in refining the idea. I started thinking about what else could go on scissors. If you're cutting out anything that needs to have exact or accurate measurement, you use a ruler, protractor, and pencil. So I added the protractor. It moves along the ruler so the paper can be lined up according to the angle. To use the scissors, simply position the blade of the scissor with the desired length on the ruler, move the protractor so that the angle is lined up with that length, and cut." He was a winner at the 1997 Craftsman/NSTA Young Inventors Awards Program for his Calibrated Angle and Depth Scissors. In 1998, at age twelve, he was inducted into the National Gallery for America's Young Inventors. In 2003, Ariel and his father gained Patent No. 6,647,842 and No. 6,513,247 for Ariel's device. They are now working on plans to produce and sell his scissors. "It's a great tool for kids who are doing basic math or geometry," said Ariel. And he has proof. He made sixteen of his scissors and gave them to one of his elementary school teachers who used them in her classroom. ■

Activities

1. Be a Detective. Find Patent Numbers!

   Many items in your home or classroom have tiny patent numbers imprinted on them or noted on labels. Get out your magnifying glass and look for the numbers. (Note: "Patent Pending" or "Patent Applied For" means that the inventor has applied for a patent but has not yet received it.)

2. Do a Sample Patent Search

   Almost everyone loves ice cream cones, but if you don't eat them quickly, the ice cream drips down onto your hand. Why hasn't anyone invented a better ice cream cone? Maybe they have. Do a patent search to find out. Follow the instructions on page 85 on how to look for patents using search words. Use the words *ice cream cone* for your search. (Note: If a patent relates in a small way to an ice cream cone, it may pop up in your search. For example, everything from machines for making a cone to a decorative container for holding a cone will be on the list. To more easily search for actual cone designs, read the descriptions.) What do you notice about the results? Do any of the patents have a good solution to the drip problem?

Registering a Trademark

9

While a patent protects your invention, a trademark, also called a mark, identifies the source. The mark helps you to answer "Who makes these goods? Who provides these services?" A trademark can be a word, a logo, or a slogan about a product or a company. Amazingly, a symbol, a sound, and even a color can be a trademark. You will notice that in certain sections in this chapter, trademark symbols are used after brand names. This is simply to illustrate their use to you. In most books that you read, including this one, trademark symbols are not used after brand names.

Trademarks Are All Around You

Trademarks appear on bags, cans, bottles, packages, labels, and billboards; on the sides of airplanes or trucks; on signs; on storefronts; on uniforms and other clothing; and in many other places. You hear sounds, slogans, and jingles on TV or the radio that are trademarks. Once you start noticing them, you'll see and hear them everywhere.

Companies establish trademark rights for their names so that no other business can use those names for the same products or services. The idea is that customers become familiar with a product, a service, or a place and with its trademark. Customers associate a trademark with the quality of a product or a service and base their decision to purchase, use, or visit it again on that. This makes trademarks valuable.

The U.S. Patent and Trademark Office registers trademarks, helping to protect both the business owner and the consumer.

Trademark Symbols

Look at the name on a toy, a bag of food, or a clothing label. Notice the ® or the ™ next to the name or the image. The ® and the ™ indicate a trademark. Anyone can claim rights to a mark by using ™. Only after it is registered with the federal government can someone use ®. If an application has been filed, but the trademark registration has not yet been granted, the ™ must be used.

Companies can own several trademarks. A trademark can be different from the formal name or the trade name of a company. Dungeons & Dragons® is the registered trademark of a role-playing game, which is a product of the company Wizards of the Coast, Inc. Monopoly® is a registered trademark for the board game, a product of Hasbro, Inc. Wham-O Inc.'s products include Frisbee Toss™ and Tidal Wave™.

Inventor's Tip

"If you have a great name for your product, a trademark may be the way to go. They are not very expensive, and they can come in very handy."

—Chris Haas, inventor of the Hands-On Basketball

Common or generic terms that are used as names for products cannot be trademarks. For example, "computer strap" and "TV stand" merely describe a type of product and do not identify any particular manufacturer or source.

Common words can be used as part of a trademark, but the common words are not trademarks. For example, Hands-On Basketball™ is a product of Sportime®. Yet since the word *basketball* is common, the following disclaimer is listed on the U.S. Patent and Trademark Web site: "No claim is made to the exclusive right to use 'basketball' apart from the mark as shown."

Types of Trademarks

Most trademarks are product or company names. PlayStation® is the name and the trademark of a game product. TOYS "R" US® is the name and the trademark of a company.

Trademarks can visually tell people that a certain company is selling a product. They make something easy to recognize. A trademark can be a logo. According to *Webster's Encyclopedic Unabridged Dictionary*, a logo is a graphic representation or symbol of a company, a name, or a trademark, abbreviation, and so on designed for easy recognition. IBM, for International Business Machines Corporation, is an example. A red cross is a logo for the Red Cross international rescue organization. A symbol or a character can also be a trademark. The "swoosh" is the symbol of the Nike Company. The Doughboy is the character trademark of the Pillsbury Company, and Red, Blue, Green, and Crispy are the spokes-candies of the M & M's® Brand Chocolate Candies of Mars, Inc.

Colors can be trademarks. The trademark for McDonald's golden arches includes both color and shape.

Trademarks can be slogans about a particular product or a company. Hear a slogan, think of a company or a product. That is the idea. "I'm Lovin' It®" is a registered trademark of the McDonald's Corporation, yet the company, like other companies, introduces new slogans all the time. "Jump Rope for Heart®" is a slogan of the American Heart Association. "Eat Fresh®" is a slogan of the Subway restaurant chain. These slogans suggest something about the product or the experience of people who use it.

Sometimes sounds can be trademarks as well. An example of this is the NBC chimes.

Applying for a Trademark

Trademarks are used in business. Unless you're in business to sell a product or a service, you cannot establish a trademark. Let's say that you're selling your invention, to your friends or the general public. To establish a trademark, you would decide on a mark and begin to use it. Your rights to a trademark start the first time you use the mark. You can think up a name, a visual image, or a slogan and begin to use this trademark for your invention, as long as it's not already being used.

How to Do a Trademark Search

To do a trademark search online, follow these simple steps.

1. Go to the U.S. Patent and Trademark Office Web site home page (www.uspto.gov).
2. Look on the left for Trademarks. Click on Search.
3. You are on the Trademark Electronic Search System (TESS) page. Click on New User Form Search.
4. In the space after Search Term, type in the name of a trademark (such as Hands-On Basketball). Click on Submit Query.
5. A list of records of trademarks will appear. To the right of the trademark is the term Live or Dead. *Dead* means the trademark is no longer registered, but it doesn't necessarily mean that the mark can be used, because a business somewhere might still be using it. Common law rights allow use by that party. If you used the trademark, you'd be violating that business's rights. (If only one trademark exists, then all of the information pertaining to that trademark will appear.)
6. If no trademark exists, the following message will appear: "Sorry, no results were found for your query."

Some other search tips include (although searches will work with any number of words, I used two in my examples for simplicity):

- If you put " " around two words, the search will retrieve only trademarks that use the exact phrase, for example—"Hands-On."
- If you search for two words using "and" in between the words (for example, "hands and on"), the search will retrieve trademarks using both of those words, but not necessarily in that order, and there may be other words in between, such as "on my hands."
- If you search for two words using "or" in between the words, for example, "hands or on," the search will bring up every trademark using either of those words.

To discover whether someone else is using the same trademark or one so similar to the one you want to use that customers might confuse the two, you can check magazines, telephone books, and catalogues for other marks that are currently in use. You also can do a search on the U.S. Patent and Trademark Office's database (www.uspto.gov) to see whether anyone has applied to register a mark you've chosen or a confusingly similar mark. (If you plan to sell your invention, it's a good idea to have a trademark lawyer do these searches, because it's hard to pull up all of the possibly similar marks.)

If you do a search of publications online and don't find a confusingly similar mark, it's a good bet that you can use your choice for a trademark if you start a business. Then, when you begin using your mark, write ™ next to it.

You can also apply to register your trademark with the federal government. The process costs several hundred dollars, which is much cheaper than a patent application. Trademark applications include

- your name and address
- a drawing of the trademark
- a listing of the goods and the services that the trademark will be associated with
- a filing fee

Trademark applications can be done online or by mail. The United States Patent and Trademark Office (USPTO) encourages trademark applications to be done online. The site is user-friendly, and each part of the application has a help section.

If you apply to register a trademark, attorneys at the Patent and Trademark Office will examine your application. They'll compare it to currently registered trademarks or other marks in prior-pending applications. If no similar marks exist and other legal requirements are met, your mark may be registered. Your mark will have to be renewed every ten years while it is being used.

If trademarks are continuously used and maintained by people in business, they can be renewed indefinitely and will last for the life of the business. Many trademarks have been used for fifty, sixty, and even a hundred years.

A person or a business with a trademark, whether or not it is registered, can take legal action if another business uses a similar name or image. Although there is no requirement to register a trademark, this formality provides the owners with certain legal advantages. For example, a court will assume that the registrant owns the mark and has the exclusive right to use the mark nationwide or in connection with the goods or the services listed in the registration. The infringement of a federally registered trademark can result in the guilty party paying damages and attorneys' fees.

Trademarks instead of Patents

Sometimes inventors choose the trademark route so that they can quickly jump into the marketplace. A patent is costly, and the invention may not be patentable. Also, it can take several years to gain a patent. In the meantime, the inventor will establish his or her product and business name by advertising the trademark.

Sometimes an inventor doesn't seek a patent in order to avoid revealing a secret ingredient in a product. This is called a trade secret. Patents require full disclosure, revealing every ingredient and giving full instructions so that others can make the product after the patent expires. A company that doesn't want to reveal a trade secret would not choose to apply for a patent. It can establish its product by advertising. For example, Coca-Cola has a secret ingredient. Because the company didn't want to reveal the secret ingredient, it didn't apply for a patent. Instead, it registered its trademarks for Coca-Cola and used the trademarks in advertisements so that people recognized the soda by its trademark. Even after numerous colas were produced by other companies, many people stuck with the Coca-Cola brand.

Another way that a trademark can benefit an inventor is when the inventor can't obtain a patent. Maybe a patent was granted years ago for a similar idea, or perhaps the idea is an old one. For example, the creators of the Hula Hoop couldn't get a patent because the toy is thousands of years old. Children in ancient Egypt made circular hoops out of grapevines and played with them in the same way we do today. During the fourteenth century, a "hooping" craze swept England and was popular among adults as well as kids. The word *hula* was attached to the toy in the early 1800s, when British sailors visited the Hawaiian Islands and noted the similarity between "hooping" and hula dancing. But the name Hula Hoop was new and could be registered as a trademark.

> ### Inventor's Tip
>
> "Boinks! were a hit from the start. Having a trademark is important in the toy business. We got one right away to establish our toy. As my mom says, 'If you have a hit, protect it.'"
>
> —*Colleen Murphy Zeppos, inventor of Boinks!*

The Hands-On Basketball

In the third grade, Chris Haas, of Murrietta, California, played a lot of basketball. When he got an assignment to create an invention that would help people do something better, he thought about kids who didn't know how to play the game well. So he created a new type of basketball. It has handprints that show kids where to hold the ball to shoot a basket. Chris's teacher, friends, and family thought it was a great idea and encouraged him to sell it.

His family turned to a patent consultant to see about patenting his idea. "I was told that a patent would not be of great use to me because other companies could slightly change my product to get around the patent," said Chris. They decided to go the trademark route. "Our family was throwing around names one day, just kind of joking, and I said 'Hands-On Basketball,' and it kinda stuck," said Chris. He protected his idea by registering a trademark that identified his product: Hands-On Basketball®.

Chris Haas with the Hands-On Basketball.

Chris and his dad spent about a year creating a prototype for the Hands-On Basketball. They experimented with various colors and types of handprints and decided to use neon-yellow balls with orange stripes, plus the handprints. They put together a brochure about their basketball, went to the library to research companies that might be interested in selling the product, found thirteen companies to approach, and sent out letters with the brochures.

Chris remembered the next stage. "When we got the letters back and companies said they didn't think it would ever be anything, it was hard, but my family kept encouraging me." A year and a half later, Chris's father, who was a coach at Chris's school, got a call at the school. Chris was in the fourth grade then. "I went to Chris's classroom," said Mr. Haas, "and we had the call transferred." They both listened while a representative of Sportime, a company that sells sports equipment, told them that it was interested in making and selling the ball.

Chris and his family signed a contract with Sportime, giving the company exclusive rights to produce and sell the basketball and to use the trademark Hands-On Basketball. "Since then," said Chris, "many other companies have been interested in my hands-on ideas, but they haven't wanted to proceed without the use of the trademark. I couldn't allow that because of my contract," he said. "It goes to show how important a name can be."

Since the 1990s, Sportime has sold hundreds of thousands of Chris's Hands-On Basketball all over the world. In addition, Chris registered a trademark for the name Hands-On Football for a football with handprints that is also sold by Sportime. "It's a really great feeling to walk into a store and see my products," said Chris. "It was a great experience, not just because it's making money, but it's helping kids around the world, and that's awesome." ■

Activities

1. Design a Trademark

   Choose a familiar trademark and redesign it. Use different colors and types of letters or shapes. Or design a trademark for your own invention. Draw your design by hand or use a computer.

2. Create a Character

   Many companies use animal characters or fantasy figures to advertise their products: Tony the Tiger, the Trix rabbit, and so on. Think of an animal character or a fantasy figure for one of your favorite products or for your own invention and draw a picture of it. Explain how it relates to your product.

3. Write a Slogan

   Try writing a slogan for a product or for your own invention. As you work on it, consider the following questions: How does the invention make people feel? How can it help them? What words best describe it? The answers can help you to create a short, snappy slogan.

10

Manufacturing, Packaging, and Selling an Invention

Think about why you buy one product instead of another. Did you see it on a commercial? Hear about it from a friend? And once you are interested, what do you look for in a product? Does it look cool? Does it seem like it will last a long time? Will it be fun, or will it help you solve a problem? Everyone thinks about these things when deciding whether to purchase a product. If you want to turn your invention into a product that will sell, you have to consider all these issues and more.

The Secret Camera Journal

When eight-year-old Sara Elias Rodriguez's teacher asked her to paint a picture of her idea for a cool toy, she painted a secret camera hidden in a copy of *Little Red Riding Hood*, one of her favorite books. "I love spy movies," admits Sara, "and I've seen spies with cameras in lots of things but never in a book." Her teacher sent her drawing, along with those of her classmates, to the Kid Inventor Challenge sponsored by Wild Planet Toys, Inc. "I didn't think I'd win," said Sara. "There were kids in my class with really good ideas." Sara's idea was picked out of the thousands that were submitted.

After the selection, she and her family were invited to the Wild Planet offices so that Sara could advise the company on how to develop the secret camera book into a product. The Secret Camera Journal that she and the others developed is not a book but a notebook with a camera inside, which also includes a photo album and a secret compartment. "I sent my idea in when I was eight and now I'm ten and the product is just coming out. It can't just be done in five minutes," said Sara. ∎

Sara Rodriguez working with Tricia Wright of Wild Planet on the Secret Camera Journal.

You need to answer many questions before your invention hits the shelves. For example: Will anyone be interested in buying it? Is it safe? How much will it cost to produce? What kind of package would attract the most customers? Would you sell more products if games or activities were included?

As inventors and other people work at turning an invention into a product, they look to try to figure out answers to all these questions. Think of ways to make your product appeal to more people.

Auto-Off Candle

Lisa Wright, of Columbus, Ohio, created the Auto-Off Candle, a candle that turns off automatically. "Both my grandma and my mom have left candles burning and started burning the countertops," said Lisa. When she was trying to think of something to invent, her mom, Connie, said, "Maybe you can invent a candle that goes out by itself."

Lisa, then a student at Arts Impact Middle School, talked to her sixth-grade science teacher, Mr. D'Aurora, who suggested that she use bits of metal around the wick. "I tried metal washers, metallic tape, and sinkers. They all worked," said Lisa. "When the candle burned down to the metal, it went out automatically."

So Lisa and her dad, Mike, worked together and made models of her idea. They used a candle mold to form several candles and inserted pieces of metal at different levels along the wick. Lisa timed how long it took for each candle to burn; then, with that information, she made candles that would automatically go off after fifteen minutes, thirty minutes, or an hour. She won first place at her school invention competition and was one of ten students invited to participate in Bridge the Gap, an entrepreneurial program of the Winners League Foundation of Columbus, Ohio. The purpose of the program was to help young inventors explore the steps of turning an invention into a product.

Lisa, the other students, and some of their parents visited

- A factory, where products are made.

- A law office, where they heard about patents and trademarks.

- A graphic arts studio, where graphic artists showed how they help inventors package their products to be more appealing to customers.

- An advertising firm, where they found out how advertisements are designed for magazines and commercials made for radio and TV.

Lisa Wright displays her Auto-Off Candle.

"It was a learning experience for both me and my dad," said Lisa. "We learned something new every week." In 2002, at age fourteen, Lisa was inducted into the National Gallery for America's Young Inventors. ∎

Many other programs exist for students to learn about manufacturing and other aspects of business. Sometimes they are offered through schools or by local or national organizations. Check out the Web sites listed in the appendix for more information.

Product Development

If you want to turn your invention into a product, start by thinking of ways to make it more appealing to customers, so that it's a 'gotta have' product. Two eight-year-old boys from Highland Park, Illinois, got an idea for a toy in a flash and then spent a lot of time developing it into a product they could sell.

KIDS INVENTING!

Flip-Itz

"Matt and I were at a basketball banquet, just hanging out, really bored, hungry," said Justin Lewis. "When the pizzas came, we saw this three-legged plastic stand that was in the box and thought, 'Cool.' Then we pushed it down, and it flipped up. The other kids at our table looked in their pizza boxes, and then they started playing with their stands." Matt Balick added, "Before we knew it, kids at all the other tables were doing it." The two had made a toy out of a pizza box lid support. They showed their parents and said, "This could be a great toy."

"I'm in marketing," said Matt's dad, Robert Balick. "I saw what they were doing, and I talked to Justin's father, Cort, who is a businessman. We decided to go for it." The four of them, Justin, Matt, Robert, and Cort, became a team. "We started brainstorming about what these little things could really be," said Robert. They decided to call them Flip-Itz and registered the name as a trademark.

Next, they had to create a toy. "We couldn't just buy pizza box stands and add faces," said Cort. "The pizza box stands weren't designed to be toys." The team decided to redesign the stands so that faces were on top and the legs flared out and were longer. You could press down on the face to make the toy flip. With these changes, they looked more like toys and could represent characters with names like Gorilla Gus or Slapshot. Each character was made in a different bright color and had a different flexibility. "My favorite was Webber the Spider," said Matt, "because it flew the highest."

Manufacturing the toy was their next challenge. The team looked for a company with experience in manufacturing small plastic items. "Some plastics would break when you pushed down on the toys," said Cort. "Other plastics were too soft, so the toys wouldn't fly. With other plastics, the toys would fly too high. Other plastics were too stiff. Others just didn't feel right. We finally found the right combination of plastics to make the toys so that they would fly high enough, flip, and have the right feeling in the fingers," he added. "And then we had to have them checked for safety."

Next, they created games. "Flip-Itz 21 is my favorite," said Justin. "If it lands on its feet, that's five points. If it lands on its side, that's one point. Upside down, three points. And," he added, "Flip-Itz Golf is really fun 'cause you can get the whole family involved."

Their next step was to choose the packaging. How many Flip-Itz should they put in one package? What should the package say on the front and the back? They decided to put four Flip-Itz in a see-through plastic container on a card. It sold for $2.49. The card was also a hanger that could easily be displayed in a store. On the back of the card were suggestions for how to play games with the toys, with a reference to a Web site where you could play virtual Flip-Itz and learn about the characters.

Flip-Itz were a hit. The toys sold for several years. Along the way, the boys were featured in many newspapers and even on TV. "In the end, it was a great experience for Matt and Justin," said Robert. "We hope we instilled in them the idea that anything is possible." ■

Matt Balick (left) and Justin Lewis (right) playing with their Flip-Itz toys.

Manufacturing any product can be complicated. Sometimes one company can't do the whole job. A product might have to be manufactured at several different companies. That's what one young inventor discovered.

Boinks! and Boinks! Buddies

Meghan Murphy, of Bloomfield Hills, Michigan, grew up in a family that makes and sells Boinks! The Pocket Rocket, a toy invented by her older sister, Colleen. One day Colleen and their brother, Kevin John, were in the garage, where they started to play with scrap pieces of automobile tubing insulation. Their dad, Kevin, who worked in the automotive business, had left the tubing out. The woven pieces were about as light as a feather. Colleen scrunched a piece of one, let it go and it flew! Then she and her brother aimed pieces at each other. "It was so much fun," explained Colleen.

Colleen started sharing the "toy" with other people. "Her friends would ask if they could have some to use as party favors or stocking stuffers," said Colleen's mother, Joyce Murphy. "We were hand cutting them with a heat cutter, then it dawned on us that we could sell them." They registered a trademark: Boinks!™.

Meghan watched all this while she was growing up. Boinks! was a simple scrunchy toy that had to be manufactured by three different companies. The automotive insulation, the material Colleen played with, was flat and black. It came on a spool, like a string or thread. Boinks! are not flat or black. They are colorful, round tubes. How did they get that way?

1. First, the Murphys went to the company that made the black automotive insulation and special ordered it to be manufactured in red at first, then later in pink, yellow, green, blue, and other bright colors.

2. Next, they had another company use a machine that would pressurize and heat the flat material so that the Boinks! would expand and become a tube.

3. Finally, the job of cutting the Boinks! into 5-inch pieces was done by another company—one that had the proper cutting tools.

When Meghan was thirteen, she went with her parents to a trade fair. While her parents sold Boinks! at their booth, Meghan wandered around looking at toys in the other booths. "I saw a bunch of bendable-foam pens with character heads on top in a booth of a Chinese company," said Meghan. "The character heads were brightly colored and made in lots of different shapes. Some were flat. Some had feathers. Others were like airplane wings with eyes. Others were like rockets."

Meghan had studied Chinese, a language offered by her school. "When I met the man in the booth, right away I knew he was from China, so I tried to talk to him a little bit," said Meghan. "I showed him the Boinks! and we played with them. Then I tried putting some of the character heads on top of a Boinks! to see if it would fly. It worked."

Meghan had an idea. Put a character head onto Boinks! to make Boinks! Buddies—a Boink! with a head. Would kids buy it? Would her parents manufacture it? Could it be sold alongside Boinks!? Her parents weren't sure.

Meghan had to convince her parents that Boinks! Buddies was a good idea. She decided to ask people whether they liked her new idea for a toy. She drew up a survey about the Boinks! Buddies and presented it to students at her high school, where she was taking a business class. She presented the same survey to the kids she babysat. The two groups became her focus groups—the name for a group of people that give opinions about a product. She asked them simple questions, such as, "Which characters and colors do you like best?" and "What would you pay for a Boinks! Buddy?"

Meghan found that certain colors and characters were more popular than others and that people would pay a fair price. When she presented the results to her parents, they thought it would be worth the investment to manufacture Boinks! Buddies.

Meghan Murphy with some Boinks! Buddies.

Then Meghan really began to learn about manufacturing. "Before we made the Boinks! Buddies, I thought we would just make them when we could," she said. Then she discovered that it was more complicated; people in business work together as a team. "It's not easy to figure it out," said Meghan. "It was confusing at first. There are so many people involved. The stores that order the toys, the companies that make and assemble them, and the ones that package and ship them. Things have to be done on time. There are deadlines. Even for the first step, if we're a day late, it can mess everything up."

Boinks! have sold for seventeen years and Boinks! Buddies for four. "It was nice to learn from my mom," said Meghan, who, at age eighteen, received the "Future Entrepreneur" scholarship from the National Association of the Self-Employed (NASE) in 2003. ∎

THE NATIONAL ASSOCIATION FOR THE SELF-EMPLOYED (NASE), founded in 1981, represents hundreds of thousands of small businesses—those headed by self-employed owners with five or fewer employees. Since 1993, NASE has annually granted a Future Entrepreneur Award and other scholarships supporting the philosophy of entrepreneurship, rather than a specific profession. College-bound freshmen who are dependents of NASE members are eligible to apply. Check out www.nase.org for more information.

Find the Right Company to Manufacture Your Invention

If you want to find a company to make your invention, don't pick just any manufacturing company. Find one that makes products like yours. If a company primarily makes plastic products and your invention will be made of metal, you wouldn't choose that company.

You also need to protect your idea when you present it to a potential manufacturer. Before talking to the company representative, ask the individual to sign a non-disclosure agreement. A non-disclosure agreement basically stipulates that the other party will keep the invention a secret. A representative of the company signs it and agrees not to talk about the idea with others or to make the product. Many companies also have their own version of a non-disclosure agreement. (Specifics about non-disclosure agreements are available in many business or invention books.) If you tell the company your idea and you don't have a confidentiality agreement, one established by the signed non-disclosure agreement, the company could use your idea.

To find potential companies, check out the information included in the *Thomas Register of American Manufacturers*. It is available in book form in most libraries, or go to www.thomasregister.com. It is a comprehensive resource for finding companies and products manufactured in North America.

Selling Your Invention

Young inventors usually don't sell their inventions on their own. Most often, they do it with their families. Some kid inventors and their families create companies to sell the inventions. Other families help the inventors license their inventions.

Sometimes young inventors do projects for school and then end up selling their inventions, even though they hadn't planned on it. That can happen in cases where the inventors create simple, low-cost inventions. Their models are usually the type that can easily be used by others.

No Loss Lacrosse

Kaitlin Fairweather, of Amherst, New Hampshire, was twelve and in sixth grade when she created a practice accessory for lacrosse. When Kaitlin practiced on the grass behind her house, she sometimes lost the ball in the woods behind her house. Since each ball costs $2.50, losing them soon got expensive. She found a small net bag, put a lacrosse ball in it, and attached a piece of elastic cord to the bag. Then she fastened the other end of the cord with a clip onto her lacrosse stick. If she threw the ball out, it would bounce right back.

"The whole idea was to not lose the ball," said Kaitlin, who called her invention No

Loss Lacrosse. She used the name as part of her slogan: No Loss Lacrosse: One Ball, No Problems. She used the same theme in a jingle as well:

"Why waste your time looking for the ball?
With No Loss Lacrosse you won't look at all . . ."

Kaitlin's first model had a 10-foot cord. To see how it would work for someone older and stronger, she asked a high school varsity lacrosse player to test it. The cord broke. She used a thicker elastic cord, but the ball bounced back too fast. Realizing that inexperienced players wouldn't be able to respond so quickly, she experimented with length and decided on a 12-foot cord. The improved version worked for both inexperienced and experienced players. Then she improved the bag by finding one made of Teflon-coated mesh that wouldn't tear with constant use. When she presented No Loss Lacrosse at her school invention fair, she had what amounted to a finished product, one that she could use—and did!

She didn't win any awards, but a lot of her friends wanted a No Loss Lacrosse when they saw hers. Kaitlin and her mom, Sarah, decided to make about six dozen and sell them at a lacrosse tournament. They sold out in two hours. "People said, 'Sell it on the

*Kaitlin Fairweather with her
No Loss Lacrosse invention.*

Web,'" said her mom, "but making the bags was labor intensive." Kaitlin added, "We were buying our materials at full price in the store and that made it more expensive than it would be if a company could buy in bulk and bring the cost of materials down."

When Kaitlin was doing research to find out whether No Loss Lacrosse was an invention, she became familiar with companies that might be interested in licensing it. Since one of the companies, Brine Inc., a major lacrosse equipment company, was located in nearby Massachusetts, she made an appointment to see its representatives. When she and her dad met with them, Kaitlin took her model and the display board that she'd used at the invention fair to demonstrate how No Loss Lacrosse worked. She explained its effectiveness and how popular it was with her fellow players.

A company director expressed interest in licensing it if Kaitlin could get a patent, so Kaitlin's dad and one of his business associates, who was a patent attorney, obtained a patent and also registered the trademark: No Loss Lacrosse™. "Some of my friends can't really believe it," said Kaitlin. "It's kind of crazy. It's still hard to grasp, but it's cool to say I've invented this." Kaitlin's invention is now marketed as the Brine Ball Returner, a product sold exclusively by Brine Inc. Kaitlin's trademark No Loss Lacrosse™ appears on the package as well. ■

Licensing Your Invention

Kaitlin's family decided not to form a company to sell her invention. Instead, they contracted with a company to make and sell her invention for them. That's called licensing. With licensing, you allow a company with experience and the right machinery to use or sell your invention for a period of time and pay you for the right to do so. Licensing contracts can be confusing, but the main points are

- Licensing or selling the rights to an invention to one company for a period of time is called an exclusive license. If you sell the rights to several companies, which means that all the companies can sell your invention at the same time, it's a nonexclusive license.

- In most licensing contracts, the inventor is paid a royalty, which means that the amount of money he or she gets depends on how many units of the product are sold. Royalties might be 5 percent or more of the selling price. For example, if a company sells 40,000 units of a product based on your invention, and each unit sells for $10, your 5 percent royalty would be $20,000.

- Royalty payments are made according to a set schedule, perhaps once, twice, or three times a year.

Inventor's Tip

"Go with your idea. Take advice if you think it will work, but stay true to what you think and what you want. Even if you have problems, you can overcome them if you just stay with it. Any little idea can become something huge and worthwhile."

—Kaitlin Fairweather, inventor of No Loss Lacrosse

- In some contracts, inventors ask that a company make its best efforts—do the best job that it can—in selling the product.

- Some contracts require a company to sell a certain number of units per year for the license to continue.

Finding companies that might want to sell your invention is almost like locating a company to manufacture it. Look at products like yours in a store and note the names of the companies that make them. You can also check lists of companies in magazines, in catalogues, or on the Internet to discover which ones make products that resemble yours. If your invention is a toy, focus on toy companies that make similar toys. If your invention is related to sports, check out sports equipment companies. If it's a learning game, check out educational companies or game companies.

You could do research at your local library to find the names and the contact information for companies that might be interested in either selling or producing *and* selling your invention. Several sources include lists of companies and information about whether a company is successful or barely surviving. Check out these three:

1. *Thomas Register of American Manufacturers*—Although this multivolume book lists manufacturers, it also lists companies that not only manufacture but also promote and sell products. Visit www.thomasregister.com.

2. *Standard & Poor's Register of Corporations*—It provides company information in books and online at www.standardandpoors.com. Here, you can find out whether a company you are interested in is doing well financially.

3. Dun & Bradstreet—This company has a database on millions of companies. Check out companies in its books or at www.dnb.com/us/.

Once you have a list of companies, you can write each one a letter that mentions its existing products and explains how your invention would fit in with its product line. You should ask the company, "What is your standard policy for submitting new products? If you have one, can you let me know what it is? If you do not, I am enclosing a non-disclosure agreement for you to sign so that I may reveal my product to you." Some inventors also use the word "Confidential" on all letters and documents that they send to companies.

Oops! Proof No-Spill Bowl

Alexia Abernathy, of Cedar Rapids, Iowa, got the idea for inventing a no-spill bowl for toddlers by watching her babysitter's two-year-old son try to carry his cereal bowl while walking. "He was at that independent stage," said Alexia, "and the cereal and milk would just slosh and end up spilling. So I came up with the idea of hot gluing a small plastic bowl inside a bigger one," she said. The larger bowl had a lid. She cut the center out of it, then snapped it back on the outer bowl. The cereal and the milk in the small inner bowl would splash into the large bowl as the boy walked, and the lid prevented everything from spilling out of the large bowl.

At Invent Iowa in 1992, the fifth-grader's no-spill bowl won an award and was a crowd favorite. Alexia discussed her product's success and its possible future with her parents. "We talked about what it takes to get it on the market," said Alexia. While Alexia's dad is an attorney, he is not a patent attorney, so he called a friend of his who was a patent attorney. "He said, 'Well, patents cost $5,000. There are a lot of people out there with patents who have no product. Why spend the money if you can't sell your product?'" Alexia explained.

An advertisement for Alexia Abernathy's Oops! Proof No-Spill Bowl.

In order to find companies that might buy her invention, Alexia and her dad visited local stores, looked at products for kids, and put together a list of fourteen companies. Then, Alexia, with her father's help, wrote letters to them. "I started out trying to get their attention," said Alexia, who is now in college. "I wrote, 'Hi, I'm Alexia Abernathy, and I'm an eleven-year-old inventor.'" To protect her idea, and following the advice given by the patent attorney, the letter didn't reveal very much about the bowl but requested companies to contact her if they wanted to know more.

Over the next year, she got replies. "I wasn't sitting around watching my mailbox," said Alexia, "but almost all the companies responded. Some, especially the big companies, said, 'We absolutely can't do this because we have our own inventors.' Probably fifty percent of them said, 'Hey, we like your idea. Can you give us some more information?'"

When Alexia wrote a second letter to the interested companies, she and her father included a non-disclosure agreement. If the companies did not agree to it, the Abernathys didn't send them any additional information. To the interested companies that did agree, they sent photos of the invention and explained how it worked. She and her dad kept records of the letters. If any company produced a bowl like hers, it would be suspicious.

About half of these companies wanted a little more information, so Alexia made a videotape of herself demonstrating the bowl. "I was my own little spokesperson," she said.

Little Kids, Inc., an East Providence, Rhode Island, children's products manufacturer, decided to license what would become the Oops! Proof No-Spill Bowl. Alexia and her father signed an agreement with the company, and they applied for a patent. When Patent No. 5,366,103 was granted on November 24, 1994, the day of Alexia's fourteenth birthday, Alexia assigned the patent (the right to use the invention) to Little Kids, Inc. The company sold more than forty thousand of the bowls from 1994 to 1997, with sales of over $100,000. ∎

Inventor's Tip

"I created my bowl as a school project. It was just a side thing, but it turned into this amazing opportunity that really opened up some unique paths for me. You never know the outcome unless you try."

—Alexia Abernathy, 1996 inductee into the National Gallery for America's Young Inventors for the Oops! Proof No-Spill Bowl

Activities

1. Figure Out Whether You Could Sell Your Invention

   a. Price Your Invention

   One of the first steps in determining whether you can sell your invention is to figure out what it costs to make and how much you could charge for it. Start by adding up the cost for materials. Next, estimate how long it will take to make one item or unit. Give yourself the minimum wage. Add the two costs, plus a profit. What do you think? Is it a reasonable price?

b. Form a Focus Group

Let's say you've created a terrific invention and made a really good model. Who would like to buy your product? In other words, who is your target audience? Kids? Elderly people? People who play a certain sport? Assemble a small group—a focus group—made up of your target audience. Show them your model. Let them hold it or use it. Check out their reactions. Then ask them some questions, such as

- Do you like the way it looks? The color? How would you change it?
- Would you buy it if you saw it in a store? For yourself? As a gift?
- How badly do you want it? On a scale of 1 to 10, with 10 being the highest, how would you rate it?
- How much would you pay for it? (Compare that to the price you determined.) Or ask them whether they would pay what you determined to be a fair price.

Their reactions may help you to redesign your invention or may encourage you to think about selling it.

2. Design an Advertising Campaign for a Favorite Product or for Your Own Invention

- Design an ad. You've seen a zillion ads for products in magazines and newspapers. Find ones that appeal to you and use them as models. Then, create an ad for your own invention. Include a photo or a drawing, a slogan, and reasons why someone should buy the product.
- Design a package. Make it look great. Include a name, a visual image, and a slogan on the package.
- Do a thirty-second radio spot.
- Write a jingle.

Appendix A:
Suggested Reading

Caney, Stephen. *Invention Book*. New York: Workman, 1985.

Casey, Susan. *Women Invent! Two Centuries of Discoveries That Have Shaped Our World*. Chicago: Chicago Review Press, 1997.

Elias, Stephen, and Kate McGrath. *Trademark: How to Name Your Business and Product*. Berkeley, Calif.: Nolo Press, 1992.

Hitchcock, David, Patricia Gima, and Stephen Elias. *Patent Searching Made Easy: How to Do Patent Searches on the Internet and in the Library*. Berkeley, Calif.: Nolo.Com, 1999.

Jones, Charlotte Foltz. *Mistakes That Worked: 40 Familiar Inventions and How They Came to Be*. New York: Doubleday, 1991.

Kassinger, Ruth. *Reinvent the Wheel: Make Classic Inventions, Discover Your Problem-Solving Genius, and Take the Inventor's Challenge*. New York: John Wiley & Sons, 2001.

Knapp, Zondra. *Super Invention Fair Projects: How You Can Build a Winning Invention*. Los Angeles: Lowell House Juvenile, 2000.

Lo, Jack, and David Pressman. *How to Make Patent Drawings Yourself*. Berkeley, Calif.: Nolo Press, 2003.

Mariotti, Steve. *The Young Entrepreneur's Guide to Starting and Running a Business*. New York: Three Rivers Press, 2000.

Platt, Richard. *Smithsonian Visual Timeline of Inventions*. New York: Dorling Kindersley, 2001.

Pressman, David, and Richard Stim. *Nolo's Patents for Beginners*, 3rd edition. Berkeley, Calif.: Nolo Press, 2002.

Sobey, Ed. *How to Enter and Win an Invention Contest*. Berkeley Heights, N.J.: Enslow, 1999.

Thimmesh, Catherine. *Girls Think of Everything*. New York: Houghton Mifflin, 2000.

Tomecek, Stephen, and M. Stuckenschneider. *What a Great Idea: Inventions That Changed the World*. New York: Scholastic, 2003.

Tucker, Tom. *Brainstorm! The Stories of Twenty American Kid Inventors*. New York: Farrar, Straus and Giroux, 1995.

VanCleave, Janice. *Science Project Workbook*. Hoboken, N.J.: John Wiley & Sons, 2003.

Wilson, Antoine. *Be a Zillionaire: The Young Zillionaire's Guide to Distributing Goods and Services*. New York: Rosen Publishing Group, 2000.

Wulffson, Don L. *The Kid Who Invented the Trampoline and More Surprising Stories about Inventions*. New York: Dutton Children's Books, 2001.

Appendix B:
Useful Web Sites

About.com (inventors.about.com/od/firststeps/) This site has stories about young inventors, links to pages about inventors of all ages and countries, and a lot of information about becoming an inventor.

Activities for Young Inventors (inventors.about.com/cs/kidactivities/) This site features a list of links to Web sites for the young inventor and great sites about inventions.

Bill Nye the Science Guy (www.billnye.com) Bill Nye provides questions and answers about science, as well as demos and information.

By Kids For Kids (www.patentcafe.com/discovery_cafe/index.html or www.bkfk.com/) This company hosts a club for kids, an online magazine, and links to many resources for young inventors. The company has arranged licensing for a variety of kids' inventions (featured on its Web site).

International Federation of Inventors (www.invention-ifia.ch/ifiayouth.htm) This site provides information about invention programs for youths around the world.

InventorEd, Inc. Presents: Kids Inventor Resources (www.inventorEd.org/k-12) This assortment of links to inventor resources for kids was created by Ronald J. Riley, an independent entrepreneur, consultant, and advocate of American invention.

Lemelson-MIT Program (web.mit.edu/invent/) Visit this site to learn about inventing, inventions, the accomplishments of young and adult inventors, as well as to find games, links to other sites, and information on programs and grants offered by the Lemelson-MIT Foundation.

Macrothesaurus (users.erols.com/cohcnjosh/120600inve.html) This Internet directory lists inventor associations and forums around the world, funding sources, publications, and other resources for inventors.

The National Gallery for America's Young Inventors (www.pafinc.com/) This online museum is dedicated to preserving and promoting great inventions produced by America's youths. Six young people in grades K through 12 are inducted annually.

Profiles of women inventors (inventors.about.com/cs/womeninventors/)

Profiles of black inventors (inventors.about.com/od/blackinventors/)

U.S. Patent and Trademark (www.uspto.gov/) This official site provides information about patents and trademarks. Patent and trademark searches can be done on the site. Check out the Kids' Pages for games, puzzles, and activities.

Junior Achievement (www.ja.org) This organization operates in nearly a hundred countries. In partnership with business and educators, the organization uses hands-on experiences to help young people understand the economics of life.

BizTech Online Entrepreneurship Program (www.nfte.com) This online interactive course offers fun, easy-to-follow chapters, timed quizzes, real-life profiles of well-known entrepreneurs, "cyber field trips," and an online BizPlan and BizGame. The point of all the activities is to help you build a business plan. (There is a $20 fee.) The course is presented by the National Foundation for Teaching Entrepreneurship (NFTE), whose mission is to teach entrepreneurship to young people ages eleven through eighteen.

Appendix C: Invention Competitions, Programs, and Camps

State Programs

Connecticut Invention Convention (CIC)

P.O. Box 230311
Hartford, CT 06123-0311
www.ctinventionconvention.org

The CIC, which began in 1983, is a nonprofit educational organization dedicated to the goal of promoting critical and creative thinking. The statewide program is open to Connecticut's schoolchildren in grades K through 8. It is financed entirely through corporate and private donations and made possible by an all-volunteer board and staff. Various awards are presented by the CIC and other organizations.

Invent Iowa State Invention Convention

Tel: (800) 336-6463 (toll-free)
E-mail: clar-baldus@uiowa.edu
www.uiowa.edu/~belinctr/special-events/inventia

This competition is open to students in grades K through 12 who live in Iowa. It is coordinated by the Connie Belin & Jacqueline Blank Center for Gifted Education and Talent Development and is sponsored by the Belin-Blank Center at the University of Iowa, the Colleges of Engineering of the University of Iowa and Iowa State University, the Iowa Intellectual Property Law Association, Iowa Biotechnology Association, and Rockwell Collins. Awards for the top state inventors include scholarships and merit awards of $50 savings bonds. The program and the free curriculum are available for use by other interested organizations.

New Hampshire Young Inventors Program (YIP)

24 Warren Street
Concord, NH 03301
Tel: (603) 228-4530
Fax: (603) 228-4730
E-mail: info@aas-world.org
www.aas-world.org

Established in 1986, YIP is a program of the Academy of Applied Science, a private nonprofit organization, incorporated in 1963. It is open to students in grades K through 8. The academy has entered into a collaboration with the Lemelson Center at the Smithsonian Institution's National Museum of American History to establish a national presence for the Young Inventors' Program.

Competitions for Teams

Christopher Columbus Awards

E-mail: success@edumedia.com
www.christophercolumbusawards.com

This program is sponsored by the Christopher Columbus Foundation in cooperation with the National Science Foundation. With the help of an adult coach, sixth- through eighth-grade students work in teams of three or four, identify a community issue, and use science and technology to develop an innovative solution by doing research and consulting with experts, who include scientists, businesspeople, and legislators. Prizes include all-expenses-paid trips for eight finalists' teams and their coaches to Walt Disney World to attend National Championship Week, plus a $200 grant to further develop their ideas. Two teams receive a $2,000 U.S. savings bond and a plaque for each team member, along with a plaque for their school. One team will receive a $25,000 grant as seed money to help bring its idea to life in the community.

eCybermission

E-mail: missioncontrol@ecybermission.com
www.ecybermission.com

This is an online competition sponsored by the U.S. Army that asks students to use math, science, and technology to solve a community problem. It's open to students enrolled in either 6th, 7th, 8th, or 9th grade at a U.S.-based public or private school, a Department of Defense school abroad, or a U.S.-based home school and home-schooled students taught by U.S. citizens. Prizes include U.S. savings bonds ranging in value up to $5,000.

ExploraVision

Toshiba/NSTA ExploraVision Awards
1840 Wilson Boulevard
Arlington, VA 22201-3000
Tel: (800) EXPLOR9 (toll-free)
E-mail: exploravision@nsta.org
www.exploravision.org

This is a competition sponsored by Toshiba and the National Science Teachers Association. It's open to students in grades K through 12 and asks participants to study a present technology, envision its future, and present their findings on Web pages. Each member of a winning team receives a U.S. savings bond worth, at maturity, $10,000 (first place) or $5,000 (second place), and national finalist team members and their parents travel to Washington, D.C., in June for ExploraVision Awards Weekend. There are regional and honorable mention prizes, and every student who submits an entry receives a gift.

InvenTeams

The Lemelson-MIT Program
Massachusetts Institute of Technology
77 Massachusetts Avenue, Room E60-215
Cambridge, MA 02139
Tel: (617) 253-3352
E-mail: inventeams@mit.edu
www.inventeams.org

This is a national Lemelson-MIT Program that provides grants of up to $10,000 to teams of high school students working with teachers and industry mentors. The program asks students to identify a problem that they want to address with an invention and then provides the funds to develop a prototype.

TOYchallenge

9170 Towne Center Drive, Suite 550
San Diego, CA 92122
www.toychallenge.com

This contest is open to teams of kids in grades 5 through 8 in the United States and its territories. Astronaut Sally Ride, along with Smith College and Hasbro, sponsors the contest. Teams must have three to eight members (at least half of them must be girls) and must work with a coach—a teacher, a businessperson, or a community member—who is at least eighteen years of age. The goal is to create and design an interactive learning toy or game. Five teams at each Regional Showcase will receive $250 to go toward showing off their toys at the National Showcase. Three grand prizes will be awarded, including a trip to Space Camp, the creation of personalized Hasbro figures in their likenesses, and a Thames & Kosmos Fuel Cell Car and an Experiment Kit for each team member.

Competitions for Individuals

Challenge List

c/o Partnership for America's Future Inc.
80 W. Bowery Street, Suite 305
Akron, OH 44308-1148
Tel: (330) 376-8300
Fax: (330) 376-0566
E-mail: pafinc@ameritech.net
www.pafinc.com/students/challenge.htm

This is a program for which participants must be members of the administering organization, the Partnership for America's Future Inc. (The organization also coordinates the National Gallery for America's Young Inventors.) Challenges include problem areas that would benefit by invention, such as bike safety at night, unwanted birds, and so on. Challenges may also be calls for noninvention activities, which include explanations of educational concepts. Winners who create an idea for a new way to demonstrate an educational concept may receive royalties on their ideas, if they are chosen for inclusion in the *Frey Scientific Catalog*.

The Craftsman/NSTA Young Inventors Awards Program

National Science Teachers Association
1840 Wilson Boulevard
Arlington, VA 22201-3000
Tel: (888) 494-4994 (toll-free)
E-mail: younginventors@nsta.org
www.nsta.org/program/craftsman

This program began in 1996 and is open to students in grades 2 through 8 who live in the United States or its territories. The program challenges students to invent or modify a tool that makes life easier. Twelve national finalists receive a $5,000 U.S. savings bond, as well as a trip to the national awards ceremony. Other winners receive bonds valued at $250 to $500.

Invent America! Student Invention Contest

United States Patent Model Foundation
Invent America!
P.O. Box 26065
Alexandria, VA 22313
Tel: (703) 942-7121
Fax: (703) 461-0068
E-mail: inquiries@inventamerica.org

This competition, hosted by Invent America!, a nonprofit educational program of the United States Patent Model Foundation, is open to students in grades K through 8 whose schools or families have purchased its curriculum kits. Prizes include U.S. savings bonds and an award certificate.

Inventive Kids Around the World Contest

Inventive Women Inc.
401 Richmond Street W, Suite 228
Toronto, Ontario, Canada M5V 3A8
www.inventivekids.com

Sponsored by Canada's Inventive Women, Inventive Kids hosts a yearly contest calling for inventions in a variety of categories, including safety, health, the environment, and everyday living. It's open to children ages seven through twelve. The kids who submit the top three ideas in each challenge win an Inventive Kids T-shirt and a "Great Idea!" certificate and have their winning entries featured on the Inventive Kids Web site.

The Kid Inventor Challenge (K.I.C.)

Wild Planet's Kid Inventor Challenge
P.O. Box 194087
San Francisco, CA 94119-4087
www.wildplanet.com
www.kidinventorchallenge.com

Hosted by Wild Planet Toys Inc., this is a contest for kids, ages six to twelve, who live in the United States or Canada (excluding Quebec). Kids are asked to invent a nonviolent toy by drawing a picture of the toy and writing a brief description. A hundred entrants are selected to be toy consultants for a year. They receive toys and are asked to comment on them. A few kids have their ideas made into toys sold by Wild Planet.

Student Ideas for a Better America

c/o Partnership for America's Future Inc.
80 W. Bowery Street, Suite 305
Akron, OH 44308-1148
Tel: (330) 376-8300
Fax: (330) 376-0566
E-mail: pafinc@ameritech.net
www.pafinc.com

This is a monthly contest open to students (grades K through 8 and 9 through 12) and is sponsored by the Partnership for America's Future, a nonprofit organization that also sponsors the National Gallery for America's Young Inventors. Students are asked to think of a new way to demonstrate an educational concept or an idea for a new product (or an improvement for an existing product or procedure). The best student idea in each division (K through 8 and 9 through 12) each month wins $100. Winning entries may be eligible for induction into the National Gallery for America's Young Inventors, or, if chosen for inclusion in the *Frey Scientific Catalog* (on pages 1–5), students will receive royalties.

Awards

The National Gallery for America's Young Inventors

Partnership for America's Future Inc.
80 W. Bowery Street, Suite 305
Akron, OH 44308-1148
Tel: (330) 376-8300
Fax: (330) 376-0566
E-mail: pafinc@ameritech.net
www.pafinc.com
www.pafinc.com/gallery/index.htm

This is a museum of young American inventors. The National Gallery inducts six young people in grades K through 12 annually. Each applicant must have won a national invention competition, be a patent holder, have a patent pending for his or her invention, or have a product based on the invention that is being sold in stores nationwide. Awards include the permanent display of the invention, a trip to the awards ceremony, and U.S. savings bonds.

Science Fairs and Competitions—for Individuals or Teams

The Discovery Channel Young Scientist Challenge (DCYSC)

Science Service
1719 N Street, NW
Washington, DC 20036

Tel: (202) 785-2255

www.sciserv.org or www.discovery.com/dcysc

This is a middle school science competition created by Discovery Communications, Inc., in partnership with Science Service. Every year, more than sixty thousand children from around the country enter their science projects in one of the science and engineering fairs affiliated with Science Service. Six thousand middle school entrants are then nominated by their fair directors to enter their projects in the Discovery Channel Young Scientist Challenge—the only competition of its kind for students in grades 5 through 8.

The Intel International Science and Engineering Fair (Intel ISEF)

Science Service
1719 N Street, NW
Washington, DC 20036
Tel: (202) 785-2255
www.sciserv.org

Founded by Science Service in 1950, this is the world's largest precollege celebration of science. Every year, more than a million students in grades 9 through 12 compete in regional science fairs and nearly five hundred Intel ISEF–affiliated fairs held around the world. More than thirteen hundred finalists from approximately forty nations win the chance to compete in fourteen categories for over $3 million in college scholarships, internships, cash prizes, and science-themed trips. The top prize is the Intel Young Scientist Award, which includes a $50,000 college scholarship. Intel Corporation has been the title sponsor since 1996.

Intel Science Talent Search (STS)

Science Service
1719 N Street, NW
Washington, DC 20036
Tel: (202) 785-2255
www.sciserv.org

Each year, more than fifteen hundred students accept the challenge of completing an entry for the Intel Science Talent Search, with finalists competing for the top prize, a $100,000 college scholarship. Eligible students include high school seniors in the United States and its territories and American students attending school abroad. The top award in this prestigious competition, created in 1942, is often called the junior Nobel Prize.

The Siemens Westinghouse Competition in Math, Science & Technology

Siemens Foundation
170 Wood Avenue South
Iselin, NJ 08830
Tel: (877) 822-5233 (toll-free)
Fax: (732) 603-5890
E-mail: foundation@sc.siemens.com

This competition is open to high school students. It is administered by the College Board and funded by the Siemens Foundation. Students submit research reports either individually or in teams of two or three members that are judged by impartial panels of research scientists from leading universities and national laboratories. Winners of regional competitions receive an invitation to advance to the national competition in Washington, D.C. The top individual and team winners receive college scholarships of $100,000. Runners-up receive college scholarships ranging from $10,000 to $50,000. Regional winners receive prizes ranging from $1,000 to $6,000.

Camps

Camp Invention

221 South Broadway
Akron, OH 44308-1505
Tel: (800) 968-4332
Fax: (330) 849-8528
E-mail: campinvention@invent.org

This is a weeklong summer day camp offered in more than forty-five states for children in the second through sixth grades. It is a joint program of Invent Now and the National Inventors Hall of Fame.

Kids Invent Toys!

Kids Invent!
1662 E. Fox Glen Avenue
Fresno, CA 93720
Tel: (559) 434-3046
Toll Free: (866) KIT-KIDS ([866] 548-5437)
Fax: (559) 278-5914
E-mail: info@kidsinvent.com
www.kidsinvvent.com

These are one-week summer camps for elementary and middle school children in many states. Check the Web site for invention learning activities.

Camps for Girls

EXITE (Exploring Interests in Technology and Engineering Camp)

www.ibm.com/us (search the site for EXITE Camps)
Tel: (800) IBM4YOU

These one-week camps are part of IBM's Women in Technology K–12 Program, which was designed to encourage girls' interest in math and science. Sessions are held in countries around the world. The camps provide hands-on activities, ranging from designing Web pages to working with laser optics and robots.

Sally Ride Science Camp

www.sallyridecamps.com

These hands-on one-week camps focus on different scientific areas for girls in sixth through eighth grades; they are held in California and Georgia.

Science Technology and Engineering Preview (STEPS) Summer Camp for Girls

One SME Drive
P.O. Box 930
Dearborn, MI 48121-0930
Tel: (313) 271-1500
www.sme.org

This camp was initiated by the Society for Manufacturing Engineers (SME), in conjunction with the University of Wisconsin–Stout. It was replicated in Minnesota and Michigan, and camps are being planned for other states. STEPS offers a one-week introduction to the world of science, technology, and engineering for sixth-grade girls living in certain states. It is tuition-free and the campers live on-campus.

Tech Trek Camps

www.aauw-ca.org/program/techtrek.htm

These camps are sponsored by the American Association of University Women.

A host of other camps sponsored by companies and organizations encourage kids to develop skills and knowledge of math, science, and technology.

Programs

These include curriculums for camps or invention programs that can be purchased for use by groups, families, organizations, or institutions.

Energy Power Camp

c/o Partnership for America's Future Inc.
80 W. Bowery Street, Suite 305
Akron, OH 44308-1148
Tel: (330) 376-8300
Fax: (330) 376-0566
E-mail pafinc@ameritech.net.
www.pafinc.com/energy/index.htm

This camp sponsors a curriculum for a weeklong program aimed at sixth- through eighth-graders. It is offered by the Partnership for America's Future, the organization that coordinates the National Gallery for America's Young Inventors. The focus is on learning about portable power and designing portable power devices, as well as learning about invention and entrepreneurship.

Invent America!

United States Patent Model Foundation
Invent America!
P.O. Box 26065
Alexandria, VA 22313
Tel: (703) 942-7121

Fax: (703) 461-0068
E-mail: inquiries@inventamerica.org
www.inventamerica.com/contest.cfm

This is a nonprofit educational program of the United States Patent Model Foundation. The program, aimed at grades K through 8, was launched in 1987. Schools or families can purchase curriculum kits that feature handbooks with step-by-step help for kids so that they can develop invention projects. Kits also include contest entry forms for the national Invent America! Student Invention Contest.

Invention Convention

www.eduplace.com/science/invention

This is a Web site presented by Houghton-Mifflin Publishing Company, which outlines how to have an invention convention and provide guidelines on every aspect of the process. (Note: invention convention is a term that is also used by many schools and organizations that host an invention program.)

Inventive Thinking Curriculum Project (also called Project)

www.uspto.gov/web/offices/ac/ahrpa/opa/projxl/invthink/invthink.htm

This is an outreach program of the United States Patent and Trademark Office. The project is online and available for use.

Inventucation

c/o Partnership for America's Future Inc.
80 W. Bowery Street, Suite 305
Akron, OH 44308-1148
Tel: (330) 376-8300
Fax: (330)376-0566
E-mail: pafinc@ameritech.nct
www.pafinc.com/

This program, which is available to schools, has two components: learning about invention and hands-on activities. The curriculum and the components can be set up permanently at a school, or program representatives can travel to a school to conduct the program as a two-week workshop.

Meant to Invent

c/o New Hampshire Young Inventors Program
24 Warren Street
Concord, NH 03301
Tel: (603) 228-4530
Fax: (603) 228-4730
E-mail: info@aas-world.org
www.aas-world.org

This is a curriculum for grades K through 8 that is used by the New Hampshire Young Inventors Program, sponsored by the Academy of Applied Science. This organization has entered into a collaboration with the Lemelson Center at the Smithsonian Institution's National

Museum of American History to establish a national presence for the Young Inventors' Program. The curriculum is available to other organizations.

Young Inventors Program

c/o Success Beyond the Classroom
4001 Stinson Boulevard N.E., Suite 210
Minneapolis, MN 55421
Tel: (512) 638-1500
E-mail: cmac@ecsu.k12.mn.us
www.ecsu.k12.mn.us/yif or www.successbeyond.org

This is the curriculum used by the Invent Iowa statewide program. It is available for purchase by other organizations.

Index

Abernathy, Alexia, 112–114
ACE Mentor Program, 80
acronyms, 54, 55, 56
Active Spin Control, 45–46
Adams, Christina, 38–39
Adams, Dalton, 53
advertising campaign, designing, 115
Allergen Scanner, 12
alliteration, 52
Amazing Kids!—Amazing Mentors!, 80
Ameer, Alyse, 12
American Sign Language Translator, 76–77
Andersen, Ole, 87–88
Anderson, Joel, 44–45
Anderson, Mary, 82
applying
   competitions and programs, 58–65
   for patent, 90–91
   for trademark, 97–98
Armitage, Betsy, 52
Automated Page-Replacing Contrivance, 8–9
Auto-Off Candle, 103–104
Avalanche Search and Survey Helicopter, 12

Baby Buzzer, 53
Bader, Luke, 24, 27–29, 39, 53
Balick, Matt, 105–106
Bath Butler, 67
Bell, Alexander Graham, 82
Bendable Broom, 52
bicycle, 4
Big Array System, 70–71
Biodegradable Disposable Diaper, 16–17
Bodylski, Johnny, 41–42, 57

Boinks! and Boinks! Buddies, 106–108
Boogie-2-Boogie, 10
Borden, Peter, 18, 65
brainstorming, 5, 20–21, 73
breaking problem into smaller parts, 5–7
Bridge the Gap!, 104
Brown, Rachel, 66

Cactus Makes Perfect, 54
Calibrated Angle and Depth Scissors, 92–94
Camp Invention, 65, 125
camps, 65, 125–126
Cardio-Mate, 13
Carthritis, 53
Cast Cooler, 27
Celle, Kai, 67
Challenge List, 121–122
characters, creating, 101
Charlie's Automatic Dog Washer, 50–51
Chavez, Seth, 11
Chlorine Sensor, 77–78
Cho, Christopher, 8–9, 65
chores, making easier, 4–5
Christiansen, Matthew, 44
Christopher Columbus Awards, 34, 69, 72, 120
Christopher Columbus Foundation Community Grant, 12
Chu, Allan, 10–11
claims, 90–91
Clement, Lindsey, 5, 30–32, 46
Coca-Cola, 99
community problem, solving, 11–13, 73
competitions
   benefits of, 58

competitions (*continued*)
  finding, 65, 119–125
  participating in, 57–58
  preparing for, 58–59, 63–65
computers, ideas related to, 10
Connecticut Invention Convention, 119
cost estimate, 41
Craftsman/NSTA Young Inventors Awards
  program, 7, 25, 58–59, 122
Craig, Heather and Hanna, 41, 63, 79–81
Crayon Holder, 86

deadlines, knowing, 63
describing inventions, 36
design patents, 85, 88–90
discovery, finding use for, 18–20
Discovery Channel Young Scientist Challenge, 18, 123–124
display, planning, 63–64
Donovan, Marian, 5
Doucette, Michelle, 72, 73
Dun & Bradstreet, 112
Dust Storm Detector, 11

Easy Door Assist, 43
E-colocator Gloves, 53
eCYBERMISSION competition, 11, 63, 72,
  120
Edible Pet Spoon, 6
Edison, Thomas, 23, 37
Effect of Neem Oil on Mosquitoes, 18
Energy Power Camp, 126
Epperson, Frank, 50
Eubank, Katelyn, 43
EXITE (Exploring Interests in Technology
  and Engineering Camp), 125
ExploraVision Awards, 13, 63, 72,
  120–121
E-Z Gallon, 88–90

Fair Share Timer, 52
Fairweather, Kaitlin, 109–111
Farnsworth, Philo, 57
Fenugreek-Treated Paper, 18–20
Fleck, Abbey, 91–92
Flip-Itz, 105–106
focus groups, forming, 115
Friedberg, Sarah, 66, 68–69
Fry, Art, 18

Glove and Battie Caddie, 32–34
Goldstein, Cassidy, 86

Goodin, Suzanna, 6
graphic representation, 96
Greatbatch, Wilson, 14
Grip Stick, 7
guidelines for competition, reading,
  58–59
Gumball Machine, 30–32
Gurry, Bonnie, 77–78

Haas, Chris, 96, 99–101
Hall, Patrick, 44–45
Hallman, Stephanie, 69
Hands-On Basketball, 99–101
Hansen, Amy and Alyssa, 10
Hathaway Brown School, 77–78
  Outreach Student Research Program, 78
Hazen, Elizabeth, 66
HEADS UP, 54–55
hobby, improving, 7–11
Hosinski, Peter, 52
Hrabar, Kristin, 40
Hula Hoop, 99
Hunt, Patricia, 77

Ice Crawler, 79–81
ideas, getting
  brainstorming, 5
  community problem, solving, 11–13
  discovery, using, 18–20
  improvement, making, 7–11
  needs of others, meeting, 13–15
  problem to solve, looking for, 4–5
  smaller parts, breaking problem into,
    5–7
  through research, 16–18
Illuminated Nut Driver, 40
improvement, making, 7–11
infringement on patents, 91
innovations, 4
Intel International Science and Engineering Fair, 11, 124
Intellectual Property Owners, Inc., 90
Intel Science Talent Search, 17, 124
Invent America! program, 126–127
Invent America! Student Invention Contest, 32, 88, 122
InvenTeams, 12, 72, 121
Invention Convention, 13, 127
invention fairs, 57–58
inventions
  definition of, 3–4
  types of, 3–4

Invent Iowa State Invention Convention, 8, 59–61, 119
Inventive Kids Around the World Contest, 59, 122
Inventive Thinking Curriculum Project, 24–25, 127
Inventucation, 127

James, Richard, 54
Johnson, Charles, 20, 53, 55, 63
Johnson, Nicholas and Kaycee, 10
Jones, Sierra, 54
journal
   description of, 23–24
   Glove and Battie Caddie example of, 32–34
   Gumball Machine example of, 30–32
   as part of display, 35–36
   requirements for, 24–25
   Walk Along example of, 27–29
   Water Bike example of, 26–27
   witness signature in, 24
judging criteria, reviewing, 59–63

Kaonohi, Brittney, 53–54
Kellogg, Will Keith, 50
Kevlar, 16
Kid Inventor Challenge, 122–123
KidKare ride toys, 15
Kids Invent Toys!, 125
Klapman, Gabe, 70–71
Knight, Mattie, 3
Krasik-Geiger, Ariel, 92–94
Kwolek, Stephanie, 16

Land Mine Protector, 13
Lee, Hans Christiansen, 45–46
Lee, Peter Alexander, 70–71, 74
Lemelson-MIT InvenTeam Grants, 12, 72, 121
Levandusky, Steven, 34
Lewis, Justin, 105–106
Leyfert, Jodie, 12
license, exclusive, 111
licensing product, 111–112
Light Hand, 9
Litsey, Sophia, 67
Littleton InvenTeam, 71–73
log
   description of, 23–24
   Glove and Battie Caddie example of, 32–34
   Gumball Machine example of, 30–32
   as part of display, 35–36
   requirements for, 24–25
   Walk Along example of, 27–29
   Water Bike example of, 26–27
   witness signature in, 24
logos, 96
LZAC Lossless Data Compression, 10–11

Makin' Bacon, 91–92
manufacturing product, 109
marks. See trademarks
Matrix Wheelchair Seat, 38–39
Matykiewicz, Charlie, 50–51
McConnell, John, 75–76, 77
McDevitt, Ryan, 12
Meant to Invent, 127
Meggitt, Austin, 15, 32–34, 36, 52, 84, 88
MENTOR/National Mentoring Partnership, 80
mentors
   from business community, 78, 81
   as guides, 74–75
   Internet resources for, 80
   questions to ask, 81
   school programs for, 77–78
Michel, Alex, 11
Microelectrochemical Sensor and Plating System, 16
Miller, Scott, 11
Minipara, Shahid, 9
model
   cost estimate for, 41
   help, asking for, 43–45
   making, 37–39
   materials, making list of, 39–40
   scale model, making, 45, 47–49
   sketch, starting with, 39
   skills, inventorying and acquiring, 41
   tools, making list of, 40
   workshop, setting up, 42
Morlan, Krysta, 3, 26–27
Mortality Composting, 68–69
Muir, John, 4
Murphy, Colleen, 106–107
Murphy, Meghan, 105, 106–108
music, ideas related to, 9

naming invention
   catchy name, 54–55
   for feel, 53–54
   making up words, 52

naming invention (*continued*)
  for self, 50–51, 56
  for sound, 53
  for what it does, 51
  word tricks in, 52–53
National Association of the Self-
    Employed, 108
National Gallery for America's Young
    Inventors, 9, 123
National Science Teachers Association
    (NSTA), 7
needs of others, meeting, 13–15
Neem Oil on Mosquitoes, Effect of, 18
New Hampshire Young Inventors Program
    and Fair, 119–120
No Loss Lacrosse, 109–111
non-disclosure agreement, 109
nonexclusive license, 111
Now You See It, Now You Don't, 68–69
NSTA (National Science Teachers Associa-
    tion), 7

Onitskansky, Elina, 16
Oops! Proof No-Spill Bowl, 112–114
oral presentation, preparing, 64–65
O-Shock, 87–88

PaceMate, 13–14
Pasteur, Louis, 50
patents
  applying for, 90–91
  description of, 82
  granting of, 82
  infringement on, 91
  looking at, 92–93
  purpose of, 83
  trademarks compared to, 98–99
  types of, 85–90
patent search, conducting, 83–85, 94
Patterson, Brian, 11
Patterson, Ryan, 25, 38, 75–77, 78
Pearson, Daniel, 34
Pedal Powered Lawn Mower, 51
plant patents, 85, 88
Post-its, 18
Pressure Blowout Smoke Diverter, 34–35
problem to solve
  breaking into smaller parts, 5–7
  in community, 11–13
  listing, 21–22
  looking for, 4–5
product
  developing, 105–108

licensing, 111–112
manufacturing, 109
selling, 109–111, 114
turning invention into, 102–103
programs, 126–128
Pursley, John, 79, 81

Rain Watchdog, 41–42
Rastogi, Akhil, 83, 88–90
reports
  example of, 34–35
  as part of display, 35–36
research
  to determine if product exists, 20
  finding idea through, 16–18
Retractable Bicycle Fender, 8
rhyming, 52, 56
Ride, Sally, 10
Riebling, Justin, 42–43, 54
Rincon, Patricia, 44–45
Rodriguez, Sara Elias, 102
Roth, Emily, 68–69
royalties, 111
Ruff-n-Tuffies, 53–54
Rushing, Lauren, 44–45

Sally Ride Science Camp, 125
scale model, making, 45, 47–49
Schedler, Carrie, 68–69
Science Buddies online program, 80
science fairs, 57, 123–124
Science Technology and Engineering Pre-
    view (STEPS) Summer Camp for Girls,
    126
Scotchgard, 37–38
Scurci, Kathryn, 68–69
Seagreaves, Eric, 34
Secret Camera Journal, 102
Sellars, Kevin, 8, 39
selling invention, 109, 111
  Boinks! and Boinks! Buddies, 106–108
  Crayon Holder, 86
  Flip-Itz, 105–106
  Glove and Battie Caddie, 32–34
  Hands-On Basketball, 99–101
  Illuminated Nut Driver, 40
  Light Hand, 9
  Makin' Bacon, 91–92
  No Loss Lacrosse, 109–111
  Oops! Proof No Spill Bowl, 112–114
  O-Shock, 87–88
  Secret Camera Journal, 102

Sherman, Patsy, 37–38
Shukla, Kavita, 18–20, 58, 64
Siemens Westinghouse Math, Science &
    Technology Competition, 16, 124–125
signature of witness, 24
Silver, Dr. Spencer, 18
Sims, Tom, 7
Sit and Go, 6
sketching, 36, 39
skills, inventorying and acquiring, 41
Slinky, 54
slogans, 96, 101
Smith, Sam, 37–38
Snap-a-Flag, 53
Sokoloff, Harris, 54–55, 81
solution to problem
    by breaking into smaller parts, 5–7
    in community, 11–13
    looking for, 4–5
Speed Grain Cart, 42–43
Spencer, Perry L., 82
sport, improving, 7–11
Stachowski, Rich, 90–91
Standard & Poor's Register of Corporations, 112
Steinberg, Renee, 6
Stoll, Kimmy, 53–54
Stopping Cart, 44–45
Student Ideas for a Better America, 15,
    123
Sturmer, Meredith, 67
submission requirements, listing, 59
summer camps, 65
surveys, 21
Sweep Stopper, 44
symbol, 96

teamwork
    benefits of, 66
    cooperation, compromise, and, 66–69
    in large teams, 71
    planning for, 73
    in small teams, 70
Tech Trek Camps, 126
Thomas Register of American Manufacturers,
    109, 112
Tietjen, Alexa, 12
Torso Protector, 7–8
Totino, Rose, 50
TOYchallenge, 10, 72, 121
toys, ideas related to, 9–10
trademarks
    applying for, 97–98

    description of, 95
    designing, 101
    patents compared to, 98–99
    purpose of, 95
    registering, 95, 98
    symbols for, 95–96
    types of, 96–97
trademark search, conducting, 97
trade secrets, 99
Trahan, Kevin, 7–8
Trahan Torso Protector, 7–8

Underwater Walkie-Talkie, 90–91
U.S. Patent and Trademark Office, 83,
    84–85, 95, 97
utility patents, 85–88, 90–91

Vasudeva, Rishi, 16–17

Walk Along, 27–29
Washington, George, 82
Waterbike, 26–27
Web sites
    for inventors, 117–118
    for mentoring, 80
    for patent searching, 83, 84–85
    for team competitions, 72
Weiss, Mitchell, 37, 51
Western Colorado Math and Science Cen-
    ter, 77
Westinghouse, George, 3
Whale, Brandon A., 13–14
Whale, Spencer, 15
Wild Planet Toys Inc. Kid Inventor Chal-
    lenge, 9
witness signature, 24
workshop, setting up, 42
Wozniak, Steve, 10
Wright, Lisa, 103–104
Wright, Wilbur and Orville, 3, 37

Young Inventors Program and Fair (Min-
    nesota), 62, 127

Zeppos, Colleen Murphy, 99
Zordan, Alyssa, 7

Photo Credits